Welcome Home
PIES, CRISPS, AND CRUMBLES

EASY AND DELICIOUS TREATS FOR EVERY SEASON

Hope Comerford

Good Books

New York, New York

Good Books books may be purchased in bulk at special discounts for sales promotion, corporate gifts, fund-raising, or educational purposes. Special editions can also be created to specifications. For details, contact the Special Sales Department, Good Books, 307 West 36th Street, 11th Floor, New York, NY 10018 or info@skyhorsepublishing.com.

Good Books is an imprint of Skyhorse Publishing, Inc.®, a Delaware corporation.

Visit our website at www.goodbooks.com.

10 9 8 7 6 5 4 3 2 1

Library of Congress Cataloging-in-Publication Data is available on file.

Cover design by Daniel Brount
Cover photos by Meredith Special Interest Media and Bonnie Matthews

Print ISBN: 978-1-68099-756-9
Ebook ISBN: 978-1-68099-774-3

Printed in China

Table of Contents

About Welcome Home Pies, Crisps, and Crumbles

I'm so glad you've picked up *Welcome Home Pies, Crisps, and Crumbles: Easy and Delicious Treats for Every Season*! In these pages you'll find desserts for the oven, slow cooker, Instant Pot, and some that require no actual baking at all. There is quite literally something for everyone in this book.

Whether you're looking for a warm dessert like Summer Peach and Blackberry Pie, Cherry Berry Cobbler, or Peaches and Pudding Crisp, or a quick and easy dessert like Sour Cream Apple Pie or Cherry Crisp, this cookbook has you covered. Making dessert for your family or choosing a dessert to bring to a family gathering or church party just got easier! With 127 tried-and-true recipes to choose from, you can't go wrong and you won't go empty-handed!

So, are you ready to get baking? Let's do this!

Pies

Apple Caramel Pie

Sue Hamilton
Minooka, IL

Makes 8–10 servings

Prep. Time: 5 minutes ⚬ *Cooking Time: 3 hours* ⚬ *Ideal slow-cooker size: 4- to 5-qt.*

2-crust refrigerated pie dough package
2 (22-ounce) cans apple pie filling
1 teaspoon cinnamon
12 caramel candies

1. Press one crust into half the bottom of a cold slow cooker, and an inch or so up half its interior side. Overlap by ¼ inch the second crust with the first crust in center of slow cooker bottom. Press remainder of second crust an inch or so up the remaining side of the cooker. Press seams flat where two crusts meet.

2. Cover. Cook on High for 1½ hours.

3. In a bowl, mix the pie filling, cinnamon, and caramels.

4. Pour the mixture into hot crust.

5. Cover. Cook on High an additional 1½ hours.

Creamy Apple Pie

OVEN

Mary Hackenberger
Thompsontown, PA

Makes 8 servings

Prep. Time: 45 minutes ♣ Baking Time: 45 minutes

1 stick (½ cup) plus 1 tablespoon
butter, at room temperature, divided

¾ cup plus 2 tablespoons sugar, divided

1 teaspoon vanilla extract, divided

1 cup flour

1 (8-ounce) package cream cheese, at
room temperature

1 egg

4 cups thinly sliced apples, peeled or
unpeeled

½ teaspoon cinnamon

½ cup chopped pecans

1. To make the crust, use an electric mixer to beat 1 stick butter, ¼ cup sugar, and ½ teaspoon vanilla in mixing bowl.

2. Gradually add flour, until mixture forms soft dough.

3. Press into bottom and up sides of a deep-dish 9-inch pie plate.

4. In a mixing bowl, use an electric mixer to beat the cream cheese, 2 tablespoons sugar, the egg, and the remaining ½ teaspoon vanilla.

5. Spread the cream cheese mixture evenly over the crust.

6. By hand, gently mix the apples, cinnamon, and remaining ½ cup sugar.

7. Layer the apple filling evenly over cream cheese filling.

8. Dot with remaining 1 tablespoon butter. Sprinkle with nuts.

9. Make a loose tent of foil to cover the pie while baking.

10. Bake at 400°F for 15 minutes. Lower heat to 350°F and bake an additional 20 minutes. Remove foil tent. Bake 10 minutes longer, or until apples are done.

Cinnamon Apple Crumb Pie

Carol Eberly
Harrisonburg, VA

Makes 6–8 servings

Prep. Time: 10–15 minutes   *Cooking/Baking Time: 50–55 minutes*

21-ounce can apple pie filling
9-inch unbaked piecrust
½ teaspoon ground cinnamon
4 tablespoons butter, divided
1½–2 cups crushed shortbread
cookies

1. Pour the pie filling into the piecrust.

2. Sprinkle with the cinnamon. Dot with 1 tablespoon butter.

3. Melt remaining butter.

4. Place the crushed cookies in a small bowl. Stir in the melted butter until coarse crumbs form.

5. Sprinkle over the filling.

6. Cover the edges of pastry loosely with foil.

7. Bake at 450°F for 10 minutes.

8. Reduce the heat to 350°F. Remove the foil. Bake for 40 to 45 minutes, or until the crust is golden brown and filling is bubbly.

9. Cool on wire rack before cutting and serving.

Grandma's Apple Pie

Andrea Zuercher,
Lawrence, KS

Makes 8 servings

Prep. Time: 30 minutes ⚮ Baking Time: 45 minutes

6 cups pared and sliced apples (about
6 medium-sized tart apples; Granny
Smith work well)

6-ounce can frozen 100%-juice apple
juice concentrate, thawed

1½ tablespoons cornstarch

1 tablespoon water

1 teaspoon cinnamon

10-inch double piecrust, unbaked

3 tablespoons butter, optional

1. Place the sliced apples in a saucepan with the juice concentrate.

2. Bring to a boil. Reduce the heat, and then simmer, covered, for 5 minutes.

3. In a small bowl, dissolve the cornstarch in the water.

4. Gently stir into the apples.

5. Bring to a boil. Reduce the heat. Simmer, covered, for 10 to 15 minutes. Apples will begin to soften as mixture becomes thickened. Stir occasionally so it does not scorch.

6. Gently stir in the cinnamon.

7. Fill the bottom piecrust with apples.

8. Dot with butter if you wish.

9. Cover with the top crust. Pinch crusts together. With a sharp knife, cut 6 to 8 steam vents across the top crust.

10. Place the pie plate on a baking sheet in case the filling cooks out. Bake at 350°F for about 45 minutes, or until top crust is lightly browned.

Crockery Apple Pie

Ruthie Schiefer
Vassar, MI

Makes 10–12 servings

Prep. Time: 20 minutes ❧ *Cooking Time: 6–7 hours* ❧ *Ideal slow-cooker size: 4-qt.*

8 tart apples, peeled, cored, and sliced
2 teaspoons ground cinnamon
¼ teaspoon ground allspice
¼ teaspoon ground nutmeg
¾ cup milk
2 tablespoons butter, softened
¾ cup sugar
2 eggs, beaten
1 teaspoon vanilla extract
1½ cups biscuit baking mix, divided
⅓ cup brown sugar, packed
3 tablespoons cold butter

1. In large bowl, toss the apples with the spices. Spoon the mixture into a lightly greased slow cooker.

2. In separate bowl, combine the milk, soft butter, sugar, eggs, vanilla, and ½ cup baking mix. Stir to mix well.

3. Spoon the batter over the apples.

4. Place remaining baking mix and brown sugar in a small bowl. Cut cold butter into it with a pastry cutter until coarse crumbs form.

5. Sprinkle the crumbs over the batter in slow cooker.

6. Cover and cook on Low for 6 to 7 hours.

Variation:

I like to use my homemade biscuit mix instead of store-bought: 5 cups all-purpose flour, 1/4 cup baking powder, 1 tablespoon sugar, 1 teaspoon salt, 3/4 cup vegetable oil. Mix well. Store in tight container.

—Kelly Bailey

Sour Cream Apple Pie

OVEN

Carna Reitz
Remington, VA

Makes 6–8 servings

Prep. Time: 5–10 minutes ❧ *Cooking/Baking Time: 30–40 minutes*

½ cup sour cream
¼ cup sugar
1 egg
21-ounce can apple pie filling
9-inch unbaked piecrust

1. In a small mixing bowl, stir together the sour cream, sugar, and egg. Pour into the piecrust.

2. Spoon the pie filling over the sour cream mixture.

3. Bake at 375°F for 30 to 40 minutes, or until the filling is firm and the crust is slightly golden on the edges.

Variations:

You can substitute cherry, blueberry, or other fruit pie fillings for the apple filling.

Fresh Peach Pie

Lavon Martins
Postville, IA

Darlene E. Miller,
South Hutchinson, KS

Makes 6–8 servings

Prep. Time: 15 minutes ⚘ *Cooking Time: 10 minutes* ⚘ *Chilling Time: 30 minutes*

¾ cup sugar

½ teaspoon salt

1 cup water

3 tablespoons cornstarch

2 tablespoons light corn syrup

3-ounce package peach gelatin

4–6 peaches

9-inch baked piecrust

1. In a saucepan, combine the sugar, salt, water, cornstarch, and syrup. Cook until clear, stirring constantly.

2. Add the gelatin and stir until dissolved. Cool in the refrigerator for 30 minutes.

3. Slice the peaches. Place in the piecrust.

4. Pour the filling over the peaches. Chill until ready to serve.

5. Serve with whipped cream or ice cream.

Variation:

Replace the peach gelatin with strawberry gelatin. And use 1 quart strawberries, fresh or frozen, instead of the peaches.

—June S. Groff, Denver, PA

Open-Face Peach Pie

Phyllis Good
Lancaster, PA

Makes 8 servings

Prep. Time: 30 minutes & Cooking Time: 1½–2 hours
Standing Time: 30–60 minutes & Ideal slow-cooker size: 6-qt.

1 cup all-purpose flour

⅓ cup whole wheat flour

¼ teaspoon baking powder

½ teaspoon salt

2 tablespoons confectioners' sugar

4 tablespoons (½ stick) butter, room temperature

3 cups sliced fresh peaches, any juice drained off

¼ cup sugar

1 teaspoon ground cinnamon

1 egg

1 cup plain Greek yogurt

1. In a mixing bowl, combine both flours, the baking powder, salt, and confectioners' sugar. Cut in the butter with a pastry cutter or 2 knives to make fine crumbs.

2. Press crumb mixture in slow cooker to make a crust that covers the bottom and comes up 1 to 2 inches on the sides.

3. Distribute the peaches over the crust. Sprinkle evenly with sugar and cinnamon.

4. In a small mixing bowl, beat the egg. Add the yogurt and stir.

5. Pour the yogurt mixture evenly over the peaches.

6. Cover and cook on High for 1½ to 2½ hours, until the yogurt topping is firm and the crust is slightly browned.

7. Carefully remove the hot crock from the cooker and remove lid. Allow pie to rest for 30 to 60 minutes before cutting and serving. For a totally firm pie, allow to cool to room temperature.

Tip:

You may use canned peaches in place of fresh ones, but drain them very well.

Maple Peach Crumble Pie

OVEN

Judy Newman
St. Marys, ON

Makes 8 servings

Prep. Time: 30 minutes ❧ *Baking Time: 45–50 minutes*

½ cup flour
½ cup maple sugar or brown sugar
½ teaspoon cinnamon
¼ cup butter-flavored shortening
3 eggs
I tablespoon lemon juice
¼ cup maple syrup
2 (20-ounce) cans peaches, sliced and drained
9-inch unbaked piecrust
⅓ cup sliced almonds

1. In a small mixing bowl, combine the flour, sugar, and cinnamon.

2. Cut in the shortening with a pastry cutter. Set aside.

3. To make the filling, beat the eggs, lemon juice, and maple syrup together in a medium mixing bowl.

4. Fold in the peaches.

5. Pour into the piecrust. Top with the flour mixture and almonds.

6. Bake at 375°F for 45 to 50 minutes, or until set and lightly browned.

No-Bake Cherry Chilled Pie

CHILLED

Frances L. Kruba
Dundalk, MD

Makes 8 servings

Prep. Time: 20 minutes & Chilling Time: 4 hours

15-ounce can sweetened condensed milk

Juice of 2 lemons

Zest of 1 lemon

¼ cup sugar

14½-ounce can red cherries, drained

1 cup chopped nuts

2 cups whipped cream, divided

10-inch graham-cracker piecrust or 9-inch deep-dish graham-cracker piecrust

1. In a mixing bowl, mix the milk, lemon juice, lemon zest, and sugar.

2. Add the cherries and nuts.

3. Fold in 1 cup whipped cream. Pour into the piecrust.

4. Top with remaining 1 cup whipped cream. Cover.

5. Refrigerate for 4 hours before serving.

Double Crust Cherry Pie

SLOW-COOKER

Phyllis Good
Lancaster, PA

Makes 8 servings

Prep. Time: 20 minutes & *Cooking Time: 1½–2 hours*
Standing Time: 30–60 minutes & *Ideal slow-cooker size: 6-qt.*

2 (9-inch) piecrusts
2 (21-ounce) cans cherry pie filling
1 teaspoon almond extract

1. Take one of the rolled-out piecrusts and fit it into slow cooker as you would line a pie plate, bringing it up the sides 1 to 2 inches and gently pushing it into the bottom.

2. In a bowl, stir together the pie filling and almond extract. Spoon mixture into the crust in slow cooker.

3. Cut remaining crust in 1-inch strips. Lay half the strips ½ inch apart on top of the pie filling, pinching the ends gently to the bottom crust and removing excess length. Lay the rest of the strips the opposite direction in the same manner.

4. Cover and cook on High for 1½ to 2 hours, until crust is firm and getting brown and filling is hot.

5. Remove the hot crock from the cooker and set aside to cool for 30 to 60 minutes before cutting. For a totally firm pie, allow to cool to room temperature before serving.

Cherry-Blueberry Pie with Almond Streusel Topping

Becky Lumetta
Romeo, MI

Makes 12 servings

Prep. Time: 35 minutes   ⚬   Chilling Time: 2 hours
Baking Time: 50–55 minutes   ⚬   Cooling Time: 6–8 hours

1 9-inch store-bought or homemade piecrust

Filling:

¾ cup plus 2 tablespoons sugar

¼ cup cornstarch

5 cups fresh blueberries (can use frozen, do not thaw)

2 cups fresh cherries (pitted) (can use frozen, do not thaw)

2 tablespoons lemon juice

1 tablespoon almond extract

Topping:

⅓ cup almond flour

⅓ cup all-purpose flour

4 ounces marzipan or almond paste, broken into pieces

¼ cup cold, unsalted butter, cut into small cubes

½ teaspoon salt

1. Roll out piecrust on floured surface and carefully transfer to a pie plate. Turn edge under and crimp decoratively as desired, forming a ¼-inch edge above the rim of the pie plate. Refrigerate for at least 30 minutes while making filling.

2. Whisk together the sugar and cornstarch in a large saucepan. Add the fruits and lemon juice. Turn on heat and bring fruit mixture to low boil. Continue to cook over medium heat until mixture bubbles and thickens while stirring gently. This should take about 10 to 15 minutes. Remove from heat and add almond extract. Transfer to bowl and cover with plastic wrap, making sure wrap touches surface. Chill until cool, about an hour.

3. For topping: Combine all ingredients in a food processor, pulsing until the mixture just begins to form into clumps. Transfer to a bowl and chill.

4. Preheat oven to 400°F. Position rack in bottom third of oven.

5. Spread filling in prepared unbaked crust and then spread topping evenly over filling.

6. Place pie on a baking sheet and bake until filling starts to bubble thickly and topping is crispy and golden, about 50 to 55 minutes. If edges or topping starts to get too dark before filling bubbles, top with aluminum foil to slow browning.

7. Allow pie to cool completely before cutting. It is best to refrigerate overnight. Serve with ice cream or whipped cream.

Pear & Almond Cream Pie

Becky Lumetta
Romeo, MI

Makes 12 servings

Prep. Time: 35 minutes   ❧   Chilling Time: 30 minutes   ❧   Baking Time: 40–42 minutes

1 9-inch store-bought or homemade piecrust

Filling:

¾ cup plus 2 tablespoons sugar

¾ cup unsalted butter, softened

2 eggs, room temperature

1 teaspoon almond extract

1⅓ cups almond flour

2 tablespoons all-purpose flour

15-ounce can pear halves in light syrup

Sliced raw almonds

Tip:

If almonds around edge start to brown too quickly, cover edge with aluminum foil.

1. Roll out the piecrust on a floured surface and carefully transfer it to a pie plate. Turn edge under and crimp decoratively as desired, forming a ¼-inch edge above the rim of the pie plate. Refrigerate for at least 30 minutes while making the filling.

2. Preheat oven to 375°F and position rack in bottom third of oven. Prick the crust with a fork, then line the crust with parchment paper or lightly sprayed aluminum foil, fill it with baking weights, and parbake for 10 to 12 minutes until lightly browned. Allow to cool.

3. For filling, cream the sugar and butter together until light and fluffy. Add the eggs one at a time, scraping bowl after each addition. Add the almond extract. Add the almond flour and all-purpose flour. Scrape bowl and make sure all ingredients are mixed well.

4. Spread filling in cooled piecrust.

5. Drain the pear halves and arrange on top of the almond filling (you can choose to slice thinly or leave them whole; either way results in a beautiful pie!) and then sprinkle the sliced almonds around the outer edge of the pie.

6. Bake at 375°F for 30 minutes. The almond filling will puff up around the pears and become golden brown.

Lemon Pie for Beginners

OVEN

Jean Butzer
Batavia, NY

Makes 8 servings

Prep. Time: 10 minutes ☙ Cooking Time: 10–12 minutes ☙ Cooling Time: 15 minutes

1 cup sugar

4 tablespoons cornstarch

¼ teaspoon salt

½ cups water, divided

3 egg yolks, slightly beaten

2 tablespoons butter

⅓ cup lemon juice

9-inch baked piecrust

**Meringue or whipped
cream, optional:**

3 egg whites (for meringue)

¼ teaspoon cream of tartar
(for meringue)

3 tablespoons sugar (for meringue)

1. Combine the sugar, cornstarch, salt, and ¼ cup water in 1½-qt. microwave safe bowl.

2. Microwave remaining ¼ cup water on High until boiling. Stir into the sugar mixture.

3. Microwave for 4 to 6 minutes until very thick, stirring every 2 minutes.

4. Mix a little hot mixture into the egg yolks. Blend the yolks into the sugar mixture.

5. Microwave for 1 minute more.

6. Stir in the butter and lemon juice.

7. Cool for 15 minutes and pour into the piecrust.

8. If desired, top with meringue (instructions below) or serve with whipped cream.

Meringue Instructions:

1. To make a meringue, beat 3 egg whites, adding ¼ teaspoon cream of tartar and 3 tablespoons sugar slowly. Continue beating until stiff peaks form.

2. Cover the lemon filling with meringue to edge of crust.

3. Bake in 350°F oven for 10 to 12 minutes or until meringue is golden.

Tip:

Using the microwave is much easier than cooking the filling on the top of the stove. You don't have to worry about it sticking or burning to the bottom of the pan.

Lemon Pie à la Mode

Joyce Nolt
Richland, PA

Makes 8 servings

Prep. Time: 20 minutes ⚭ Cooking Time: 20 minutes
Standing Time: 30–60 minutes ⚭ Chilling Time: 3–5 hours

⅓ cup (5⅓ tablespoons) butter

⅓ cup lemon juice

¾ cup sugar

Pinch salt

3 eggs, beaten

10-inch baked piecrust

1 quart vanilla ice cream, softened

2–3 cups frozen whipped topping, thawed, or whipped cream

Tip:

Use chopped nuts, toasted coconut, or a drizzle of chocolate syrup to garnish if you wish.

1. Prepare a double boiler (or place a heatproof bowl over a saucepan of simmering water; the bowl should fit with no gap and without touching the water).

2. Place the butter in top of the double boiler to melt.

3. When the butter is melted, add the lemon juice, sugar, and salt.

4. Stirring constantly, slowly add the beaten eggs.

5. Cook in the double boiler until mixture is thick and smooth, stirring constantly.

6. Remove from the heat. Set aside to cool to room temperature, 30 to 60 minutes.

7. Spoon filling into piecrust. Cover. Freeze for 2 to 4 hours, or until firm.

8. Remove from freezer and top with softened ice cream and whipped topping. Cover tightly.

9. Return to freezer for at least an hour before serving.

Lemon Cheese Pie

CHILLED

Jere Zimmerman
West Middletown, PA

Elaine Patton
West Middletown, PA

Esther Gingerich
Parnell, IA

Makes 8 servings

Prep. Time: 10 minutes ⚜ *Cooling Time: 1 hour*

8 ounces cream cheese, softened
2 cups milk, divided
3.5-ounce box instant lemon pudding
9-inch graham cracker piecrust

1. In a good-sized mixing bowl, beat the cream cheese until soft and creamy.

2. Add ½ cup milk and blend until smooth.

3. Add the dry pudding mix and blend until smooth.

4. Blend in 1½ cups milk until well incorporated.

5. Beat slowly for 1 minute.

6. Pour into the graham cracker crust.

7. Refrigerate for at least 1 hour before serving.

Lemon Sponge Pie

Phyllis Good
Lancaster, PA

Makes 8 servings

Prep. Time: 25 minutes ♣ Cooking Time: 1½–2½ hours
Standing Time: 1–2 hours ♣ Ideal slow-cooker size: 6-qt.

9-inch unbaked piecrust

3 eggs, separated

¼ teaspoon cream of tartar

2 tablespoons butter

1 cup sugar

Finely grated zest of 2 lemons

Juice of 2 lemons

3 tablespoons all-purpose flour

½ teaspoon salt

1⅓ cups milk

1. Take the rolled-out piecrust and fit it into a slow-cooker crock as you would line a pie plate, bringing it up the sides 1 to 2 inches and gently pushing it into the bottom.

2. Beat the egg whites and cream of tartar with an electric mixer until the whites stand up in stiff peaks. Set aside.

3. In a mixing bowl, cream the butter, sugar, and egg yolks.

4. Add the lemon zest, lemon juice, flour, salt, and milk. Beat again.

5. Fold in beaten egg whites.

6. Pour mixture in pastry-lined slow cooker.

7. Cover and cook on High for 1½ to 2½ hours, until middle is set and lightly browned.

8. Remove the crock from the cooker and uncover. Allow to cool for 1 to 2 hours before slicing and serving.

Easy Lime Pie

Trudy Kutter
Corfu, NY

Janie Canupp
Millersville, MD

Makes 6–8 servings

Prep. Time: 15 minutes ⚜ *Chilling Time: 4 or more hours*

14-ounce can sweetened condensed milk (not evaporated)

6 ounces frozen whipped topping, thawed, plus more if you choose

½ cup key lime juice

Lime zest, optional

9-inch graham cracker piecrust

2 kiwifruit, optional

1. In a large mixing bowl, mix the condensed milk with the thawed dairy topping until blended.

2. Fold in the lime juice and zest and blend well.

3. Pour mixture into the crust and chill for at least 4 hours.

4. Peel kiwifruit and slice over pie just before serving, if you like. Add a dollop of whipped topping to the top of each piece when serving, if you wish.

Key Lime Pie

CHILLED

Denise Martin
Lancaster, PA

Naomi Ressler
Harrisonburg, VA

Judy DeLong
Burnt Hills, NY

Erma Martin
East Earl, PA

Jan Pembleton
Arlington, TX

Makes 8 servings

Prep. Time: 15 minutes ⚓ *Cooling Time: 2 hours*

.3-ounce box lime gelatin

¼ cup boiling water

2 (8-ounce) containers key lime yogurt

8-ounce container frozen whipped topping, thawed

9-inch graham cracker crust

1. In a large mixing bowl, dissolve the gelatin in the boiling water. Whisk in the yogurt.

2. Fold in the whipped topping. Pour into the crust.

3. Refrigerate for 2 hours.

Variations:

1. This pie is equally delicious with a reduced-fat crust, sugar-free gelatin, and nonfat yogurt and whipped topping.
—Erma Martin, East Earl, PA

2. Substitute lemon gelatin for the lime. Substitute lemon-light yogurt for the key lime. Follow all other directions above for a lemon pie.

—Jan Pembleton, Arlington, TX

Rhubarb Custard Pie

Phyllis Good
Lancaster, PA

Makes 8 servings

Prep. Time: 30 minutes ⚶ Cooking Time: 1½–2 hours
Standing Time: 30–60 minutes ⚶ Ideal slow-cooker size: 6-qt.

9-inch unbaked piecrust
2 eggs
1 cup sugar
Pinch salt
¼ teaspoon ground nutmeg
2 tablespoons flour
⅔ cup heavy cream
2½ cups diced rhubarb

1. Take rolled-out piecrust and fit it into slow cooker as you would line a pie plate, bringing it up the sides 1 to 2 inches and gently pushing it into the bottom.

2. In a mixing bowl, whisk the eggs until they no longer cling to the whisk.

3. Add the sugar, salt, nutmeg, flour, and cream. Whisk again until no lumps remain.

4. Place the rhubarb in the crust.

5. Pour the egg mixture over the rhubarb.

6. Cover and cook on High for 1½ to 2 hours or until knife blade inserted in center comes out clean.

7. Remove the crock from the cooker and uncover. Set aside for 30 to 60 minutes before slicing and serving pie, or allow to cool to room temperature for a totally firm pie.

Grandma's Spring Rhubarb Pie

OVEN

Eleya Raisn
Oxford, IA

Makes 6 servings

Prep. Time: 30 minutes ⚸ *Cooking/Baking Time: 45 minutes*

1 cup sugar
3 tablespoons flour
2 egg yolks, beaten
3 cups diced rhubarb
9-inch unbaked piecrust

1. In a mixing bowl, stir the sugar, flour, and egg yolks together until crumbly. Set aside ¾ cup of the crumbs for topping.

2. Stir the cut-up rhubarb into remaining crumbs.

3. Spoon the rhubarb mixture into the piecrust.

4. Sprinkle the reserved crumbs on top of the pie filling.

5. Bake at 400°F for 25 minutes.

6. Reduce the heat to 350°F and bake an additional 20 minutes, or until the rhubarb filling is bubbling.

7. Allow to cool before slicing and serving.

Nantucket Pie

Barbara Nolan
Pleasant Valley, NY

Makes 8 servings

Prep. Time: 10–15 minutes ⚜ *Baking Time: 45 minutes*

2 cups whole cranberries, fresh or frozen

1½ cups sugar, divided

½ cup chopped walnuts

1 cup flour

1 teaspoon almond extract

1½ sticks (¾ cup) butter, melted

2 eggs

Coarse sugar

1. Mix the cranberries, ½ cup sugar, and the walnuts.

2. Put into bottom of very well-greased 9-inch pie plate.

3. Beat the flour, 1 cup sugar, almond extract, butter, and eggs. Pour evenly over the cranberry mixture.

4. Bake at 350°F for 45 minutes.

5. Immediately sprinkle the top with coarse sugar.

New England Blueberry Pie

Krista Hershberger
Elverson, PA

Makes 8 servings

Prep. Time: 15 minutes ⚬ *Cooking Time: 12 minutes* ⚬ *Chilling Time: 1 hour*

4 cups fresh blueberries, divided
Prebaked 9-inch piecrust
1 cup sugar
3 tablespoons cornstarch
¼ teaspoon salt
¼ cup water
1 tablespoon butter
Whipped cream

1. Place 2 cups of blueberries in a baked piecrust.

2. In medium saucepan, cook the sugar, cornstarch, salt, water, remaining 2 cups blueberries, and butter. Stir continuously until thick.

3. Cool blueberry mixture for ½ hour. Pour cooled mixture over berries in piecrust. Chill.

4. Top with the whipped cream before serving.

Raspberry-Mascarpone Pie

OVEN   CHILLED

Becky Lumetta
Romeo, MI

Makes 12 servings

Prep. Time: 10 minutes   Chilling Time: 30 minutes
Baking Time: 12–18 minutes   Cooling Time: 2½ hours

1 9-inch store-bought or homemade unbaked piecrust
½ cup raspberry jam
8 ounces mascarpone cheese
½ cup heavy cream
¼ cup sugar
¼ teaspoon ground cardamom
1 tablespoon honey
Zest of 1 orange
1 pint fresh raspberries
½ cup pistachios, coarsely chopped

1. Preheat oven to 350°F.

2. Roll out the piecrust on a floured surface and carefully transfer to the pie plate. Turn edge under and crimp decoratively as desired, forming a ¼-inch edge above the rim of the pie plate.

3. Refrigerate for at least 30 minutes, then prick crust with a fork to prevent air bubbles and line with parchment paper or aluminum foil and fill with baking weights and bake until fully done, about 12 to 18 minutes.

4. Allow to cool completely, about 30 minutes.

5. After crust has fully cooled, spread the raspberry jam evenly in the bottom of the crust.

6. Mix the mascarpone cheese, cream, sugar, cardamom, honey, and orange zest until combined.

7. Gently spread the mixture evenly over the raspberry jam.

8. Garnish with the fresh raspberries and pistachios.

9. Chill before serving, about 2 hours.

Raspberry Custard Pie

Laura R. Showalter
Dayton, VA

Makes 6–8 servings

Prep. Time: 7–10 minutes ❧ *Cooking/Baking Time: 45–55 minutes* ❧ *Cooling Time: 30 minutes*

3 cups fresh black raspberries
9-inch unbaked piecrust
¾ cup sugar
3 tablespoons flour
¾ cup half-and-half
½ teaspoon cinnamon, optional

1. Wash the berries. Dry by blotting with a paper towel. Place berries in piecrust.

2. Mix remaining ingredients in a small mixing bowl until smooth. Pour over the berries.

3. Bake at 375°F for 15 minutes. Turn oven down to 300°F. Bake for 30 to 40 minutes more, or until center is set.

4. Allow to cool before slicing and serving.

Variation:

Use peaches or other berries instead of raspberries.

Mom's Fresh Fruit Pie

Stacy Stoltzfus
Grantham, PA

Jean A. Shaner
York, PA

Janet Oberholtzer
Ephrata, PA

Eunice Fisher
Clarksville, MI

Carolyn Lehman Henry
Clinton, NY

Monica ByDeley
Annville, PA

Makes 8 servings

Prep. Time: 15 minutes ❧ *Chilling Time: 4–8 hours*

3–4 cups fresh fruit of your choice: berries, peaches, or a mixture of fruits

9-inch baked piecrust

.3-ounce package strawberry gelatin (or other flavor to match the fruit)

¾–1¼ cups sugar, depending on the sweetness of the fruit

3 rounded tablespoons cornstarch

2 cups warm water

Whipped topping, optional

1. Wash and pat dry fresh fruit. Slice if necessary.

2. Arrange fruit in baked piecrust and set aside.

3. In a saucepan, mix the gelatin, sugar, and cornstarch. Add 2 cups warm water. Cook and stir until thickened and clear.

4. Pour over fruit. Refrigerate for several hours until set.

5. When time to serve, top with whipped topping if you wish.

Summertime Berry Dessert

CHILLED

Natalia Showalter
Mt. Solon, VA

Makes 8 servings

Prep. Time: 15 minutes   Chilling Time: 1–8 hours

4 ounces cream cheese, softened

¼–⅓ cup sugar

½ cup whipping cream

9-inch graham cracker crust

3–4 cups fresh blueberries, strawberries, huckleberries, or raspberries, washed and drained

1. In a mixing bowl, blend the cream cheese and sugar until well combined and creamy.

2. Whip the cream. Fold whipped cream into the cream cheese and sugar mixture.

3. Spread whipped cream mixture into graham crust. Chill until ready to serve.

4. Just before serving, top with fresh berries.

Simple Egg Custard Pie

Peggy Howell
Hinton, WV

Makes 8 servings

Prep. Time: 10 minutes ♣ *Baking Time: 25–30 minutes* ♣ *Cooling Time: 1 hour*

4 eggs
½ cup sugar
½ teaspoon salt
2 cups milk
1 teaspoon vanilla extract
9-inch unbaked piecrust
Nutmeg, optional
Cinnamon and sugar, optional

1. Mix the eggs, sugar, salt, milk, and vanilla.

2. Pour mixture into the unbaked piecrust.

3. Sprinkle with the nutmeg or cinnamon and sugar if you wish.

4. Place on lower oven rack. Bake at 425°F for 25 to 30 minutes. Center may still be a little jiggly, but it will firm up as it cools.

5. Allow to cool 1 hour before serving.

Variation:

Spread ½ can prepared pie filling (blueberry or cherry) evenly over bottom of piecrust. Slowly pour custard filling over it so as not to disturb the fruit. Bake as instructed. The fruit under the custard makes for a tasty treat!

Magic Coconut Custard Pie

Phyllis Good
Lancaster, PA

Makes 8 servings

Prep. Time: 10 minutes ♣ Cooking Time: 2–3 hours
Standing Time: 30–60 minutes ♣ Ideal slow-cooker size: 5-qt.

4 eggs
6 tablespoons butter, room temperature
½ cup all-purpose flour
2 cups 2% or whole milk
¾ cup sugar
I teaspoon vanilla extract
I cup unsweetened shredded coconut

1. In a blender, combine the eggs, butter, flour, milk, sugar, and vanilla. Whip.

2. Stir in the coconut.

3. Pour mixture into a greased slow cooker.

4. Cover and cook on High for 2 to 3 hours, until set in the middle.

5. Uncover the slow cooker and remove the crock from the cooker. Set aside for 30 to 60 minutes before slicing and serving pie, or allow to cool to room temperature for a totally firm pie.

Swiss Coconut Custard Pie

Elsie Schlabach
Millersburg, OH

Makes 8 servings

Prep. Time: 8 minutes   *Baking Time: 50 minutes*

4 eggs

¼ cup brown sugar

¾ cup sugar

1 teaspoon vanilla extract

2 cups milk

½ cup flour

½ teaspoon baking powder

6 tablespoons butter or margarine, softened

2 drops maple extract

1 cup coconut

1. Beat the eggs in a medium mixing bowl.

2. Add the sugars, vanilla, milk, flour, baking powder, butter, and maple extract. Beat for 2 minutes.

3. Stir in the coconut.

4. Pour into a greased 10-inch pie plate. Bake at 350°F for 50 minutes until center of pie is set.

Tip:

After it's baked, the crust will be on the bottom, custard in the middle, and coconut on top. An easy trick to get a pie!

Oatmeal Coconut Pie

OVEN

Karen L. Gingrich
Bernville, PA

Makes 6–8 servings

Prep. Time: 10 minutes ❧ *Baking Time: 45–50 minutes*

2 eggs
½ cup white sugar
½ cup brown sugar
1 stick (½ cup) melted butter
1 teaspoon vanilla extract
1 cup milk
¾ cup rolled oats
1 cup shredded coconut
9-inch unbaked piecrust

1. In a bowl, mix the eggs, sugars, butter, vanilla, milk, oats, and coconut.

2. Pour into the unbaked piecrust.

3. Bake at 350°F for 45 to 50 minutes, or until set in the middle.

Famous PA Dutch Shoofly Pie

SLOW-COOKER

Phyllis Good
Lancaster, PA

Makes 8 servings

Prep. Time: 30 minutes ❧ Cooking Time: 1½–2 hours
Standing Time: 30–60 minutes ❧ Ideal slow-cooker size: 6-qt.

Unbaked 9-inch piecrust

1 cup all-purpose flour

½ cup brown sugar

2 tablespoons butter, room temperature

⅓ cup blackstrap molasses

⅔ cup mild baking molasses

1 egg

⅔ cup cold water

1 teaspoon baking soda

¼ cup hot water

1. Take rolled-out piecrust and fit it into the slow cooker as you would line a pie plate, bringing it up the sides 2 inches and gently pushing it into the bottom.

2. In a mixing bowl, cut together the flour, brown sugar, and butter to make fine crumbs. Measure and set aside ½ cup crumbs.

3. In another mixing bowl, combine the blackstrap molasses, mild baking molasses, egg, and cold water. Whisk.

4. Separately, dissolve the baking soda in hot water and then add it to mixture. Whisk again.

5. Add the crumbs to the molasses mixture. Pour into piecrust in cooker. Sprinkle with reserved ½ cup crumbs.

6. Cover, adding 3 or 4 sheets of paper towels under the lid to catch condensation.

7. Cook on High for 1½ to 2 hours, until pie is puffed a bit and center is not jiggly.

8. Uncover the slow cooker and remove the crock from the cooker. Set aside for 30 to 60 minutes before slicing and serving pie.

Cointreau Pecan Pie

OVEN

Becky Lumetta
Romeo, MI

Makes 12 servings

Prep. Time: 30 minutes ⚓ *Baking Time: 45–55 minutes*

Unbaked 9-inch store-bought or
homemade piecrust

¾ cups maple syrup

¾ cups brown sugar

½ corn syrup

2 ounces (½ stick) butter

3 eggs

1 teaspoon vanilla extract

¼ teaspoon salt

2 tablespoons Cointreau liqueur

1½ cup pecan pieces

1. Roll out the piecrust on a floured surface and carefully transfer to a pie plate. Turn the edge under and crimp decoratively as desired, forming a ¼-inch edge above rim of the pie plate. Freeze for at least 20 minutes while making filling.

2. Preheat oven to 350°F and place oven rack in bottom third of oven.

3. In a small saucepan, melt the maple syrup, brown sugar, corn syrup, and butter. Bring to a boil and allow to boil for 1 minute. Allow to cool to lukewarm.

4. Whisk the eggs, vanilla, salt, and Cointreau.

5. Whisk in the maple mixture.

6. Stir in the pecan pieces.

7. Pour into the prepared piecrust and place on a baking sheet. (If desired, arrange a few whole pecans on top in a decorative design just before placing pie in oven.)

8. Bake until the pie no long jiggles when baking sheet is gently tapped, about 45 to 55 minutes. If the crust starts to brown too much, cover it with aluminum foil.

Caramel and Chocolate-Hazelnut Mousse Pie

Becky Lumetta
Romeo, MI

Makes 12 servings

Prep. Time: 35 minutes ⚜ Chilling Time: 2 hours ⚜ Standing Time: 15–30 minutes

9-inch store-bought or homemade chocolate or graham cracker piecrust

Caramel Filling Layer:

¼ cup water

1½ cups sugar

¼ cup corn syrup

1 cup heavy cream

5 tablespoons unsalted butter, softened and cubed

1½ teaspoons kosher salt

1 teaspoon vanilla extract

Chocolate-Hazelnut Mousse Layer:

3 tablespoons cold water

1 teaspoon powdered unflavored gelatin

5 ounce chocolate-hazelnut spread

1 tablespoon Frangelico liqueur

4 ounces mascarpone cheese

1½ cups heavy cream

2 tablespoons cocoa powder

3 tablespoons sugar

For Caramel Layer:

1. In an uncoated, heavy saucepan, mix the water, sugar, and corn syrup. Bring to a boil and cook over medium heat until the mixture is amber in color, swirling gently to keep the mixture cooking evenly.

2. Meanwhile, in a smaller pot, heat the cream, butter, and salt. Bring just to a scald and remove from heat. Add the vanilla and keep to the side.

3. When sugar mixture is ready, reduce the heat to low and slowly pour cream mixture into sugar, whisking gently while pouring, being very careful to avoid steam. Cook until a candy thermometer reads 245°F.

4. Take caramel off the heat and stir gently until bubbles stop, then carefully pour into prepared crust.

5. Place in refrigerator while you prepare the mousse layer.

For Chocolate-Hazelnut Mousse Layer:

1. Add the cold water to a small pot and sprinkle the powdered gelatin over the water. Allow to bloom for 5 minutes.

2. Heat the water/gelatin mixture over low heat to melt.

3. Whisk in the chocolate-hazelnut spread.

4. In a medium bowl, whisk chocolate-hazelnut mixture and Frangelico into the mascarpone.

5. Using a stand mixer or hand mixer, whip together the heavy cream, cocoa powder, and sugar until soft peaks form.

6. Fold one third of the whipped cream mixture into the mascarpone mixture until mostly combined, then fold in another third of the whipped cream, and then the final third, making sure to fully incorporate all the whipped cream mixture after the final third is added.

7. Spread the mousse mixture over the caramel layer in the piecrust.

8. Chill until the mousse layer is set.

Serving suggestion:

Garnish with whipped cream, chopped hazelnuts, and/or chocolate shavings. Allow to come to room temperature for 15 to 30 minutes before serving so caramel layer can soften.

Mock Pecan Pie

Ruth E. Martin
Loysville, PA

Makes 8 servings

Prep. Time: 10 minutes ⚘ *Cooking/Baking Time: 50 minutes*

4 tablespoons (½ stick) butter, softened

½ cup sugar

I cup light corn syrup

¼ teaspoon salt

3 eggs

¾ cup coconut

¾ cup quick oats

9-inch unbaked piecrust

1. Cream the butter in a medium mixing bowl.

2. Add the sugar gradually and cream until fluffy.

3. Add the syrup and salt; beat well.

4. Add the eggs, one at a time, beating thoroughly after each addition.

5. Stir in the coconut and quick oats.

6. Pour into the unbaked piecrust.

7. Bake at 350°F for 50 minutes until the center of the pie is not jiggly. Allow to cool before slicing.

Frosty Mocha Pie

Leah Hersberger
Dundee, OH

Makes 8–10 servings

Prep. Time: 25 minutes ☙ *Chilling Time: 4 hours* ☙ *Standing Time: 15 minutes*

4 ounces cream cheese, at room temperature

¼ cup sugar

¼ cup unsweetened baking cocoa

1 teaspoon instant coffee granules

⅓ cup milk, at room temperature

1 teaspoon vanilla extract

12 ounces frozen whipped topping, thawed

9-inch graham-cracker crust

Chocolate syrup for garnish, optional

Crushed candy bars for garnish, optional

1. In large mixing bowl, beat the cream cheese, sugar, and cocoa with an electric mixer until smooth.

2. In a small bowl, dissolve the coffee crystals in milk.

3. Stir the coffee mixture and the vanilla into the cream cheese mixture.

4. Gently fold in the whipped topping.

5. Pour into the crust.

6. Cover. Freeze for 4 hours.

7. Remove from the freezer 15 minutes before serving.

8. Drizzle with the chocolate syrup and sprinkle with crushed candy bars if you wish.

Variation:

Add 8 ounces instead of 4 ounces of cream cheese if you wish.

Tip:

This can be made ahead and kept in the freezer for up to a week, tightly covered.

Butterscotch Pie Dessert

Karen Stoltzfus
Alto, MI

Makes 12 servings

Prep. Time: 15–20 minutes ⚜ *Baking Time: 20–25 minutes* ⚜ *Cooling Time: 30–45 minutes*

1½ cups flour

16 tablespoons (2 sticks) butter, melted

¼ cup chopped walnuts

8 ounces cream cheese

1 cup confectioners' sugar

2 (3.4-ounce) packages instant butterscotch pudding

3 cups milk

1 teaspoon vanilla extract

8-ounce container frozen whipped topping, thawed

½ cup butterscotch chips

1. Combine the flour, butter, and walnuts in a mixing bowl. Press into a greased 9×13-inch baking dish. Bake at 350°F for 20 minutes. Cool.

2. In a mixing bowl, beat the cream cheese until fluffy. Beat in the sugar until creamy. Spread mixture over the crust, being careful not to pull the crust up.

3. In the same mixing bowl, beat the pudding, milk, and vanilla until thickened. Spread over the top of the cream cheese layer.

4. Spread the whipped topping over the pudding. Sprinkle with the butterscotch chips.

Variations:

1. Replace the butterscotch pudding and butterscotch chips with chocolate pudding and chocolate chips.

2. Replace butterscotch pudding and butterscotch chips with pistachio pudding and chopped walnuts.

Chocolate Pecan Pie

SLOW-COOKER

Phyllis Good
Lancaster, PA

Makes 8 servings

Prep. Time: 25 minutes ❧ *Cooking Time: 2–3 hours*
Standing Time: 30–60 minutes ❧ *Ideal slow-cooker size: 6-qt.*

9-inch unbaked piecrust

1⅓ cups (4 ounces) bittersweet chocolate, chopped

6-ounce bag chopped pecans

3 eggs

1 cup sugar

6 tablespoons butter, melted

½ cup dark corn syrup

¼ cup maple syrup

1 teaspoon vanilla extract

¼ teaspoon salt

1. Fit the unbaked piecrust into the slow cooker as you would line a pie plate, bringing it up the sides 1 to 2 inches and gently pushing it into the bottom.

2. In a small bowl, toss together the chocolate and pecans. Sprinkle the chocolate/pecan mixture evenly in the piecrust.

3. In a medium bowl, whisk the eggs and sugar. Add the butter, corn syrup, maple syrup, vanilla, and salt. Whisk again.

4. Pour the filling over the chocolate and pecans in the crust.

5. Cover and cook on High for 2 to 3 hours, until filling is set and crust is getting browned.

6. Remove the crock from the cooker, remove the lid, and set the pie aside to cool to room temperature, about 2 hours, before slicing and serving.

Mocha Pie

Phyllis Good
Lancaster, PA

Makes 8 servings

Prep. Time: 20 minutes   ⚭   Cooking Time: 2–3 hours
Standing Time: 2 hours   ⚭   Ideal slow-cooker size: 6-qt.

9-inch unbaked piecrust

2 eggs

⅔ cup heavy whipping cream

1½ cups sugar

3 tablespoons unsweetened cocoa powder

1 tablespoon instant coffee granules

4 tablespoons (½ stick) butter, melted

1 teaspoon vanilla extract

¼ teaspoon salt

1. Fit unbaked piecrust into the slow cooker as you would line a pie plate, bringing it up the sides 1 to 2 inches and gently pushing it into the bottom.

2. In a mixing bowl, beat the eggs and cream until mixture no longer clings to whisk.

3. Add the rest of the ingredients and whisk well.

4. Pour the filling into the prepared crust.

5. Cover and cook on High for 2 to 3 hours, until filling is set in the middle and crust is browning.

6. Remove the crock from the cooker, uncover, and set the pie aside to cool for 2 hours before slicing and serving.

Variations:

I adore chocolate and coffee together, so this pie is a favorite of mine. However, I bet there are ways to tinker with it. Take out the coffee and put a layer of peanut butter between the filling and the crust, add some cinnamon and cayenne for a Mexican-inspired flair, or chop up some leftover Halloween candy bars and sprinkle them in the crust before pouring in the filling.

Sugar-Free Double Chocolate Cream Pie

Peggy Clark
Burrton, KS

Makes 6–8 servings

Prep. Time: 15–20 minutes   Standing/Chilling Time 30–60 minutes

1 ½ cups milk, divided

3-ounce package dark chocolate sugar-free pudding

8-ounce container light frozen whipped topping, thawed, divided

9-inch graham cracker crust

3-ounce package white chocolate sugar-free pudding

1. In a small mixing bowl, mix ¾ cup milk with the dark chocolate pudding mix.

2. Fold half of the whipped topping into the dark chocolate pudding.

3. Place the dark chocolate pudding in crust.

4. In another small mixing bowl, mix remaining ¾ cup milk with white chocolate pudding mix.

5. Fold remaining whipped topping into the white chocolate pudding.

6. Spoon white chocolate pudding over the top of the dark chocolate pudding, being careful not to mix the two.

7. Refrigerate until ready to eat.

Mocha Chiffon Pie

Ann Bender
New Hope, VA

Makes 8 servings

Prep. Time: 15 minutes ❧ *Cooking Time: 5 minutes* ❧ *Cooling Time: 2–3 hours*

1 tablespoon plain gelatin

¼ cup cold water

3 tablespoons granulated stevia

2 tablespoons unsweetened cocoa powder

1 teaspoon dry instant coffee

⅛ teaspoon salt

1½ cups evaporated milk

8 tablespoons Extra Creamy Cool Whip

1. In a small bowl, dissolve the gelatin in the cold water.

2. Mix the stevia, cocoa powder, dry coffee, and salt in a saucepan.

3. Stir the milk into the saucepan. Heat to boiling, stirring frequently.

4. Add gelatin mixture and stir until dissolved.

5. Cool in refrigerator until mixture is slightly congealed.

6. Pour into a 9-inch pie plate.

7. Cool in the refrigerator until completely set.

8. Serve each pie wedge topped with 1 tablespoon Cool Whip.

Note:

This recipe is keto-friendly!

Fudge Sundae Pie

Deb Martin,
Gap, PA

Makes 6 servings

Prep. Time: 30 minutes & Freezing Time: 2 hours

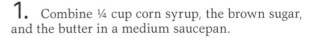

¼ cup plus 3 tablespoons light corn syrup, divided

2 tablespoons brown sugar

3 tablespoons butter or margarine

2½ cups crispy rice cereal

¼ cup peanut butter

¼ cup ice cream fudge sauce

1 quart vanilla ice cream

Tip:
Add chopped peanuts to the top, or whipped topping and maraschino cherries. Use butterscotch topping as drizzle.

1. Combine ¼ cup corn syrup, the brown sugar, and the butter in a medium saucepan.

2. Cook over low heat, stirring occasionally, until mixture begins to boil. Remove from heat.

3. Add the crispy rice cereal, stirring until well coated.

4. Press evenly into a 9-inch pie plate to form crust.

5. Stir together the peanut butter, fudge sauce, and 3 tablespoons corn syrup.

6. Spread half the peanut butter mixture over the crust. Freeze until firm, 1 hour.

7. Allow the ice cream to soften slightly.

8. Spoon the ice cream into the frozen piecrust; spread evenly. Freeze until firm, 1 hour.

9. Let pie stand at room temperature for 10 minutes before cutting and serving.

10. Warm the other half of the peanut butter mixture and drizzle over the top.

Cookies 'n' Cream Pie

Sheila Horst
Bowmansville, PA

Makes 6–8 servings

Prep. Time: 15 minutes & Freezing Time: 6–8 hours, or overnight

1½ cups half-and-half

3.4-ounce package instant vanilla, or French vanilla, pudding mix

8-ounce carton frozen whipped topping, thawed

1 cup crushed cream-filled chocolate sandwich cookies

9-inch chocolate crumb piecrust

1. In a mixing bowl, combine the half-and-half and dry pudding mix. Beat on medium speed for 1 minute. Let stand for 5 minutes.

2. Fold in the whipped topping and crushed cookies.

3. Spoon mixture into the crust.

4. Freeze until firm, for about 6 to 8 hours or overnight.

5. Remove from freezer 10 minutes before serving.

Easy Peanut Butter Pie

Kendra Dreps
Liberty, PA

Makes 6 servings

Prep. Time: 10 minutes ❧ *Chilling Time: 2–4 hours*

8 ounces cream cheese, softened

1 cup peanut butter

1 cup confectioners' sugar

8 ounces frozen whipped topping, thawed

1 graham cracker crust

Peanut butter cups, chopped, optional

1. In a large mixing bowl, cream the cream cheese and peanut butter together until smooth.

2. Stir in the confectioners' sugar until well incorporated.

3. Fold in the whipped topping.

4. Pile into piecrust.

5. If you wish, top with chopped peanut butter cups.

6. Refrigerate for 2 to 4 hours before serving.

Peanut Butter and Banana Pie

CHILLED

Jenny R. Unternahrer
Wayland, IA

Makes 8 servings

Prep. Time: 15 minutes ❧ *Chilling Time: 2–4 hours*

⅓–½ cup creamy natural peanut butter

9-inch piecrust, baked and cooled

2 bananas, sliced

3-ounce package sugar-free instant vanilla pudding

1¾ cups milk

1. Spread peanut butter on bottom and sides of baked piecrust. Use as much or as little as you like.

2. Layer the banana slices on top of the peanut butter and around the sides of the piecrust.

3. Mix the pudding and milk together according to the pudding package instructions.

4. Pour the pudding over the bananas, covering all of them.

5. Refrigerate for 2 to 4 hours, or until set.

Tip:

If you prefer a fuller pie, you can use another half package of pudding and 7 ounces milk, adding to the milk and pudding in the recipe.

Crunchy Peanut Butter Ice Cream Pie

CHILLED

Mary Ann Bowman
East Earl, PA

Susan Wenger
Lebanon, PA

Joanna Bear
Salisbury, MD

Makes 6–8 servings

Prep. Time: 15 minutes ⚘ Freezing Time: 4–6 hours

⅓–½ cup crunchy peanut butter

⅓–½ cup light corn syrup

2–3 cups crispy rice cereal

1 quart vanilla ice cream, slightly softened

Toppings of your choice: whipped topping, broken nuts, cut-up fresh fruit, mini M&M's, mini chocolate chips, or chopped peanut butter cups

Variations:

1. Instead of the corn syrup, use half a stick (¼ cup) butter and 2 tablespoons brown sugar.

2. Instead of crispy rice cereal, use 4½ cups sugar-coated cornflakes, crushed.

—Joanna Bear, Salisbury, MD

1. In a mixing bowl, beat the peanut butter and corn syrup together until well blended.

2. Stir in the crispy rice cereal.

3. Using a spoon, or your buttered fingers, press mixture into a 9-inch buttered pie plate.

4. Fill piecrust with softened ice cream.

5. Freeze for 4 to 6 hours, or until firm.

6. When ready to serve, garnish with the toppings of your choice.

7. To make serving easier, set the filled pie plate in warm water for 1 minute before cutting the pie.

Pumpkin Mousse Pie

Nadine L. Martinitz
Salina, KS

Makes 8 servings

Prep. Time: 20 minutes ☙ *Cooking Time: 1 minute* ☙ *Chilling Time: 1–2 hours*

15-ounce can pumpkin

¼ cup sugar

1¼ teaspoons pumpkin pie spice and more for garnish

½ teaspoon vanilla extract

¼ cup water

1 envelope unflavored gelatin

2½ cups fat-free frozen whipped topping, thawed, divided

6-ounce reduced-fat graham cracker crust

1. Combine the pumpkin, sugar, 1¼ teaspoons pumpkin pie spice, and vanilla in large bowl. Beat with a whisk until blended. Set aside.

2. Place the water in a small saucepan. Sprinkle the gelatin over top. Let stand until gelatin softens, about 1 minute.

3. Place the saucepan over low heat and cook, stirring continually, until gelatin completely dissolves, about 1 minute.

4. Gradually pour dissolved gelatin mixture into pumpkin mixture, beating with a whisk until blended.

5. Gently fold 2 cups thawed whipped topping into the pumpkin mixture.

6. Spread the filling in the graham cracker crust. Refrigerate until firm.

7. Fill a pastry bag with the remaining whipped topping and decoratively pipe over filling or simply drop dollops of remaining topping over pie.

8. Garnish with a few sprinkles of pumpkin pie spice.

Slow-Cooker Pumpkin Pie

SLOW-COOKER

Colleen Heatwole
Burton, MI

Makes 5–6 servings

Prep. Time: 10 minutes ❧ *Cooking Time: 3–4 hours*
Cooling Time: 2–4 hours ❧ *Ideal slow-cooker size: 3-qt.*

Nonstick cooking spray
15-ounce can solid-pack pumpkin
12-ounce can evaporated milk
¾ cup sugar
½ cup low-fat buttermilk baking mix
2 eggs, beaten
¼ stick (2 tablespoons) butter, melted
1½ teaspoons cinnamon
¾ teaspoon ground ginger
¼ teaspoon ground nutmeg
Whipped topping

1. Spray the slow-cooker crock with cooking spray.

2. Mix all the ingredients, except whipped topping, in prepared slow-cooker crock.

3. Cover. Cook on Low for 3 to 4 hours, or until a toothpick inserted in center comes out clean.

4. Allow to cool to warm, or chill, before serving with whipped topping.

Variation:

You can substitute 2½ tablespoons pumpkin pie spice in place of the cinnamon, ginger, and nutmeg.

Pumpkin Pie Dessert

SLOW-COOKER

Bonnie Whaling
Clearfield, PA

Makes 4–6 servings

Prep. Time: 15–20 minutes   Cooking Time: 3–4 hours   Ideal slow-cooker size: 5- to 6-qt.

19-ounce can pumpkin pie filling

12-ounce can evaporated milk

2 eggs, lightly beaten

Boiling water

1 cup gingersnap cookie crumbs

1. In a large mixing bowl, stir together the pie filling, milk, and eggs until thoroughly mixed.

2. Pour into an ungreased baking insert designed to fit into your slow cooker.

3. Place filled baking insert into slow cooker. Cover the insert with its lid, or with 8 paper towels.

4. Carefully pour boiling water into cooker around the baking insert, to a depth of one inch.

5. Cover cooker. Cook on High for 3 to 4 hours, or until a tester inserted in center of custard comes out clean.

6. Remove baking insert from slow cooker. Remove its lid. Sprinkle dessert with cookie crumbs. Serve warm from baking insert.

Pumpkin Pecan Pie

SLOW-COOKER

Phyllis Good
Lancaster, PA

Makes 8–10 servings

Prep. Time: 20–30 minutes ❧ Cooking Time: 1½ hours ❧ Ideal slow-cooker size: 4- or 5-qt.

2 unbaked 9-inch piecrusts

4 eggs

16-ounce can pumpkin

¾ cup sugar

½ cup dark corn syrup

1 teaspoon cinnamon

¼ teaspoon salt

1 cup pecans

1. Press the piecrusts into your cold slow cooker. Overlap the seams by ¼ inch, pressing to seal them. Tear off pieces so that the crusts fit partway up the sides, pressing the pieces together at all seams.

2. In a large bowl, beat the eggs lightly. Then stir in the pumpkin, sugar, corn syrup, cinnamon, and salt, and mix well.

3. Pour into the unbaked piecrust. Arrange the pecans on top.

4. Cover. Cook on High for 1½ hours, or until the filling is set and a knife blade inserted in the center comes out clean.

Pecan Vanilla Pumpkin Pie

Nancy Leatherman
Hamburg, PA

Makes 8 servings

Prep. Time: 15 minutes ⚬ *Baking Time: 50 minutes*

3 eggs, slightly beaten
1 cup sugar
½ cup corn syrup
1 cup cooked pumpkin
¼ teaspoon salt
1 teaspoon vanilla extract
½ teaspoon cinnamon
9-inch unbaked piecrust
1 cup chopped pecans

1. In a mixing bowl, mix the eggs and sugar.

2. Add the syrup, pumpkin, salt, vanilla, and cinnamon.

3. Beat well.

4. Pour into the 9-inch piecrust.

5. Sprinkle with the pecans.

6. Bake at 425°F for 15 minutes.

7. Reduce the heat to 350°F and bake for 30 minutes, or until set in the middle.

Yogurt Pie

Sarah Miller
Harrisonburg, VA

Shirley Sears
Tiskilwa, IL

Trudy Kutter
Corfu, NY

Betty Moore
Plano, IL

Joyce Kaut
Rochester, NY

Ruth Shank
Monroe, GA

Makes 6 servings

Prep. Time: 5 minutes & Cooling Time: 4–8 hours, or overnight

¼ cup water

.3-ounce box gelatin, your choice of flavor

2 6-ounce containers yogurt, your choice of flavor

8-ounce container frozen whipped topping, thawed

9-inch graham cracker crust

1. Boil the water. Stir in the gelatin until dissolved. Allow to cool until syrupy but not firm.

2. In a large mixing bowl, combine the partially gelled gelatin, yogurt, and thawed whipped topping.

3. Pour into the crust.

4. Allow to cool until firm, from 4 to 8 hours, or overnight.

Variation:

Skip the water and gelatin. Instead use 1 pint cut-up fruit, such as strawberries or blueberries. Mix the fruit with the yogurt and thawed whipped topping. If you use canned fruit, be sure to drain it well before mixing it with the other ingredients.

—Joyce Kaut, Rochester, NY
—Ruth Shank, Monroe, GA

Piecrust

OVEN

Christine Weaver
Reinholds, PA

Gwendolyn Chapman
Gwinn, MI

Makes 1 9-inch 2-crust pie

Prep. Time: 10 minutes

2½ cups flour
½ teaspoon salt
¾ cup shortening
6–7 tablespoons cold water

1. Place the flour and salt in a large bowl. Cut in shortening with pastry blender or 2 knives until mixture resembles coarse meal or tiny peas.

2. Add cold water a little at a time and mix lightly with fork until pastry holds together when pressed into a ball.

3. Divide dough into 2 balls, 1 using about ⅔ of the dough and the other using about ⅓ of the dough.

4. Roll out larger ball of dough on floured countertop until dough is 2 inches larger than the pie plate.

5. Lightly fold circle of dough in half. Then lightly fold in half again so that the resulting shape is a ¼ circle.

6. Lay the crust into the pie plate. Open up folds. Press the crust loosely but firmly into the plate.

7. For a prebaked shell, prick the bottom and sides of the dough with a sharp fork. Then bake the unfilled crust at 425°F for 10 minutes. If your recipe directs you to bake a filled crust, spoon or pour the filling into the crust, and then bake according to the pie recipe instructions.

Crisps

Dutch Apple-Pecan Crisp

OVEN

Becky Lumetta
Romeo, MI

Makes 9 servings

Prep. Time: 15 minutes ⚮ *Cooking/Baking Time: 40–45 minutes*

Nonstick cooking spray

1 tablespoon lemon juice

2 pounds apples, peeled, cored, and sliced

2 tablespoons all-purpose flour

¾ cups brown sugar

½ teaspoon salt

1 teaspoon cinnamon

⅛ teaspoon nutmeg

Topping:

⅔ cup all-purpose flour

⅓ cup brown sugar

⅓ cup butter

½ cup pecan pieces

1. Preheat oven to 375°F. Lightly spray an 8×8-inch baking dish.

2. Sprinkle the lemon juice over the apple slices in a large bowl

3. Mix the all-purpose flour, brown sugar, salt, cinnamon, and nutmeg. Sprinkle over the apples and toss gently to coat evenly.

4. Pour into the prepared baking dish.

5. In a food processor, blend the all-purpose flour, brown sugar, and butter. Pulse until mixture starts to resemble coarse crumbs. Add the pecan pieces and pulse once or twice to incorporate but not chop too much smaller.

6. Spread the topping mixture evenly over the apples.

7. Bake until filling bubbles, about 40 to 45 minutes. Allow to cool before serving.

Serving suggestion:
Serve with ice cream.

Pear Ginger Crisp

Phyllis Good
Lancaster, PA

Makes 4–6 servings

Prep. Time: 20 minutes ⚘ *Cooking Time: 2½ hours* ⚘ *Ideal slow-cooker size: 3-qt.*

4 large ripe pears, peeled and sliced

2 tablespoons sugar

1 tablespoon lemon juice

1 tablespoon + ½ cup all-purpose flour, divided

Nonstick cooking spray or butter for greasing slow-cooker crock

½ cup brown sugar

⅔ cup dry oats, quick or rolled (rolled have more texture)

¼ teaspoon cinnamon

Pinch ground cloves

¼ teaspoon salt

3 tablespoons cold butter

2 tablespoons minced candied ginger

1. In a mixing bowl, gently mix the pears, sugar, lemon juice, and 1 tablespoon flour.

2. Place the pear mixture in a lightly greased slow-cooker crock.

3. In same mixing bowl, cut together the remaining ½ cup flour, brown sugar, oats, cinnamon, cloves, salt, butter, and candied ginger.

4. Sprinkle oat topping over pears

5. Cover and cook on High for 2 hours, until pears are soft. Remove lid and cook on High an additional 30 minutes to crisp up the top.

Apple-Cranberry Crisp

SLOW-COOKER

Judi Manos
West Islip, NY

Makes 12 servings

Prep. Time: 20 minutes & Cooking Time: 2 6 hours & Ideal slow-cooker size: 6 qt.

3.4-ounce package vanilla instant
pudding

½ cup sugar, divided

1 teaspoon ground cinnamon

3 pounds Granny Smith apples, about
10, peeled, sliced

1 cup dried cranberries

6 tablespoons butter, melted, divided

12 vanilla wafers, coarsely chopped

¼ cup sliced almonds or pecans

1. Mix the dry pudding mix, ¼ cup sugar, and cinnamon.

2. Toss the apples and cranberries with 4 tablespoons melted butter in a large bowl. Add the pudding mixture and mix lightly.

3. Spoon into the slow cooker. Cover and cook on Low for 4 to 6 hours or on High for 2 to 3 hours.

4. Meanwhile, combine the chopped wafers, nuts, and remaining 2 tablespoons melted butter and ¼ cup sugar in shallow microwaveable dish. Microwave on High 1 minute. Stir. Microwave 1½ to 2 minutes more or until golden brown, stirring every 30 seconds. Cool.

5. Sprinkle apple mixture with cooled nut mixture just before serving.

Variations:

Can use 1 cup fresh or frozen cranberries instead of dried cranberries.

Tips:

Serve with vanilla ice cream. Add ½ teaspoon ground nutmeg. I sometimes double the vanilla wafers to 24 and the nuts to ½ cup for the topping.

Ultimate Apple Crisp

Judi Manos
West Islip, NY

Makes 6–8 servings

Prep. Time: 15 minutes & Cooking/Baking Time: 25 minutes

6–8 apples (use baking apples if you can find them)

1 cup brown sugar

1 cup dry oats, quick or rolled (both work, but rolled have more texture)

1 cup flour

1 tablespoon cinnamon

1½ sticks (12 tablespoons) butter, melted

½ stick (4 tablespoons) butter, cut in pieces

1. Core, peel if you want, and slice the apples. Place the apples in a microwave- and oven-safe baking dish (a Pyrex-type pie plate works well).

2. In a separate bowl, mix the brown sugar, oats, flour, and cinnamon. Add the melted butter and mix with a fork until thoroughly mixed.

3. Place mixture on top of the apples. Microwave on High, uncovered, for 10 minutes. Let stand for 2 minutes.

4. Place cut-up butter on top of heated apple mixture.

5. Place in oven and bake at 350°F for 15 minutes.

Grandma's Apple Crisp

OVEN

Louise Bodziony
Sunrise Beach, MO

Shelley Burns
Elverson, PA

Ruth Ann Penner
Hillsboro, KS

Darla Sathre
Baxter, MN

Makes 9 servings

Prep. Time: 20 minutes ❧ Cooking/Baking Time: 40 minutes

6–8 apples
1 cup dry quick oats
¾ cup brown sugar
½ cup flour
½ teaspoon cinnamon, optional
1 stick (½ cup) butter

1. Peel, core, and slice the apples. Place the apples in a buttered 8-inch or 9-inch square baking dish.

2. In a mixing bowl, stir together the oats, brown sugar, flour, and cinnamon if you wish.

3. Cut in butter with 2 knives or a pastry cutter until small crumbs form.

4. Sprinkle crumb topping over apples.

5. Bake at 350°F for 40 minutes, or until lightly browned.

Variation:

You can use pears, apricots, peaches, or rhubarb instead of apples.
—Ruth Ann Penner, Hillsboro, KS
—Darla Sathre, Baxter, MN

Extra Crisp Apple Crisp

Christina Gerber
Apple Creek, OH

Makes 4 servings

Prep. Time: 15 minutes ⚜ *Cooking Time: 3–6 hours* ⚜ *Ideal slow-cooker size: 6 qt.*

5–6 cups tart apples, sliced
¾ cup (1½ sticks) butter
1 cup rolled or quick oats
1½ cups flour
1 cup brown sugar, packed
3 teaspoons ground cinnamon

1. Place the apples in a lightly greased slow cooker.

2. Separately, melt butter. Add rest of the ingredients and mix well.

3. Crumble the topping over the apples.

4. Cover and cook on High for 3 hours or Low for 4 to 6 hours. Allow the cooker to sit, turned off with lid removed, for about 30 minutes before serving, so the crisp is nicely warm for serving.

Tip:

This is the recipe for people who can never get enough crisp topping on their apple crisp!

Variation:

Add 1 teaspoon salt to topping in step 2.

1-2-3 Apple Crisp

OVEN

Lavina Hochstedler
Grand Blanc, MI

Makes 8 servings

Prep. Time: 15 minutes ☙ Baking Time: 35–45 minutes

8 apples, peeled and cored
1½ cups brown sugar
1 cup all-purpose flour
1 cup quick or rolled oats
1 teaspoon cinnamon
1 teaspoon nutmeg
1 stick (½ cup) butter, softened

1. Lightly grease a 9×13-inch glass baking dish.

2. Cut the apples into slices and layer them in bottom of pan.

3. In a medium bowl, mix the brown sugar, flour, oats, cinnamon, and nutmeg.

4. Cut in the butter with a pastry blender until crumbly.

5. Sprinkle the mixture over the apples.

6. Bake at 375°F for 35 to 45 minutes, or until the top is browned.

Tip:

Because I use a glass pan, I often like to cook this in the microwave for 10 to 15 minutes before I put the crumbs on. It shortens the baking time in the oven. Bake just until the topping browns, about 15 to 20 minutes.

Spicy Sweet Apple Crisp

Phyllis Good
Lancaster, PA

Makes 6 servings

Prep. Time: 20 minutes ⚬ *Cooking Time: 3½–4 hours* ⚬ *Ideal slow-cooker size: 5-qt.*

Nonstick cooking spray or butter to grease slow-cooker crock

9 crisp baking apples, peeled or not

1 cup flour

1 cup sugar

1 teaspoon baking powder

Pinch salt

1 egg

4 tablespoons (half a stick) butter

Several shakes of roasted, or other gourmet, cinnamon

Dash or two of cardamom

1. Grease interior of the slow-cooker crock.

2. Slice the apples into the prepared slow-cooker crock, spreading them out evenly.

3. In a good-sized bowl, mix the flour, sugar, baking powder, and salt.

4. Break the egg into the dry ingredients and mix.

5. Cut the butter into chunks. Using your fingers, 2 knives, or a pastry cutter, work the butter into the dough until small chunks form.

6. Scatter chunks over apples.

7. Sprinkle apple mixture liberally with the roasted cinnamon. Add the cardamom.

8. Cover with the cooker lid. Bake on High for 3 to 3½ hours, or until firm in the middle and juices bubble up around the edges.

9. Remove the lid carefully, tilting it quickly away from yourself so no condensation drips on the crisp. Continue baking for 30 more minutes to allow the topping to crisp up.

10. Let cool until warm or room temperature before serving.

Nutty Peach Crisp

Pat Chase
Fairbank, IA

Dorothy A. Shank
Sterling, IL

Vera Campbell
Duyton, VA

Carol Lenz
Little Chute, WI

Makes 12–16 servings

Prep. Time: 5–10 minutes ❧ Cooking/Baking Time: 1 hour ❧ Standing Time: 15 minutes

29-ounce can peach slices and syrup

18¼-ounce package dry cake mix
(butter brickle, yellow, or butter pecan)

1 cup flaked coconut

1 cup chopped pecans or walnuts

1 stick (½ cup) butter, melted

1. Layer the ingredients in order listed in an ungreased 9×13-inch baking dish.

2. Bake at 325°F for 55 to 60 minutes, or until golden brown.

3. Allow to stand for 15 minutes before serving.

Serving suggestion:

Serve warm with milk, whipped cream, or ice cream, if you wish.

Apple Crunch

Anita Troyer
Fairview, MI

Makes 6 servings

Prep. Time: 30 minutes ⚜ *Cooking Time: 2½–3 hours* ⚜ *Ideal slow-cooker size: 6-qt.*

For Crock:

Nonstick cooking spray or butter

Crumb:

1 cup flour

½ cup brown sugar

½ teaspoon cinnamon

6 tablespoons butter

Filling:

6 large Granny Smith apples

½ teaspoon lemon juice

⅓ cup sugar

3 tablespoons flour

½ teaspoon cinnamon

⅛ teaspoon nutmeg

⅛ teaspoon salt

1. Spray the slow-cooker crock very well with nonstick spray, or grease the inside of the crock very well with butter.

2. Mix all the crumb ingredients. Set aside.

3. Peel, core, and cut the apples into ¼-inch slices.

4. In a bowl, mix the apples with the other filling ingredients. Dump this mixture into the prepared slow-cooker crock.

5. Place the crumb mixture over the top of the apple mixture.

6. Cover with a lid, placing a fork between the lid and the crock so that extra moisture can escape and crumbs will bake nicely. Cook on High for 2½ to 3 hours. Use care when removing the lid so that moisture on it will not drip on the crumbs.

Amazing Apple Caramel Crunch

Hope Comerford
Clinton Township, MI

Makes 4 servings

Prep. Time: 20 minutes & Cooking Time: 4 hours
Cooling Time: 1 hour & Ideal slow-cooker size. 2-qt.

Nonstick cooking spray
½ cup brown sugar
¼ cup turbinado sugar
2–3 Honeycrisp apples, cut into bite-size chunks
½ teaspoon cinnamon
½ teaspoon vanilla extract
½ teaspoon cornstarch
Dash nutmeg
Dash salt

Crumble:
⅓ cup gluten-free or regular old-fashioned oats
⅓ cup brown sugar
2 tablespoons almond flour
¼ teaspoon cinnamon
1½ tablespoons coconut oil, in solid but softened form, or butter

1. Spray the slow-cooker crock with the nonstick cooking spray.

2. Mix the brown sugar and turbinado sugar and spread the mixture across the bottom of the prepared slow-cooker crock.

3. Toss the apples with the cinnamon, vanilla, cornstarch, nutmeg, and salt. Pour evenly over the sugar mix.

4. In a bowl, mix the crumble ingredients with your fingers. Sprinkle the crumble over the apples.

5. Cover and cook on Low for 4 hours. Let sit to cool for 1 more hour, with the crock off, before serving. This will allow the caramel to thicken.

Serving suggestion:

Serve over your favorite vanilla ice cream or delicious vanilla Greek yogurt.

Healthy Coconut Apple Crisp

SLOW-COOKER

Hope Comerford
Clinton Township, MI

Makes 8–9 servings

Prep. Time: 20 minutes   &   Cooking Time: 2 hours   &   Ideal slow-cooker size: 3- or 4-qt.

Nonstick cooking spray

5 medium Granny Smith apples, peeled, cored, sliced

1 tablespoon cinnamon

¼ teaspoon nutmeg

1 teaspoon vanilla extract

Crumble:

1 cup gluten-free oats

¼ cup coconut flour

½ cup unsweetened coconut flakes

1 teaspoon cinnamon

⅛ teaspoon nutmeg

½ teaspoon sea salt

2 tablespoons honey

2 tablespoons coconut oil, melted

2–3 tablespoons unsweetened coconut milk

1. Spray the slow-cooker crock with the nonstick cooking spray.

2. In the prepared crock, combine the apple slices, cinnamon, nutmeg, and vanilla.

3. In a medium bowl, combine all of the crumble ingredients. If too dry, add a bit more honey or coconut milk. Pour the crumble over the top of the apple mixture.

4. Cover slow cooker and cook on low for 2 hours.

Serving suggestion:

Serve with a scoop of coconut ice cream.

Apple Pear Crisp

SLOW-COOKER

Phyllis Good
Lancaster, PA

Makes 8–10 servings

Prep. Time: 15–20 minutes ⚘ *Cooking Time: 2–4 hours* ⚘ *Ideal slow-cooker size: 5-qt.*

Butter to grease slow-cooker crock

3–4 large apples, unpeeled and sliced

3–4 large pears, unpeeled and sliced

½ cup sugar, or less, depending on how naturally sweet the apples are

1 tablespoon lemon juice

1 tablespoon flour

Topping:

1 cup flour

1 cup brown sugar

⅔ cup dry oats, quick or rolled (rolled have more texture)

½ teaspoon cinnamon

6 tablespoons (¾ stick) butter

1. Grease the interior of the slow-cooker crock.

2. In a big bowl, mix the apple and pear slices, sugar, lemon juice, and 1 tablespoon flour.

3. Pour mixture into the prepared slow-cooker crock.

4. In the same bowl, mix the flour, brown sugar, oats, and cinnamon. Then cut in butter with 2 knives, a pastry cutter, or your fingers. When crumbs the size of small peas form, sprinkle them over the fruit mixture.

5. Cover crock. Bake on High for 2–3 hours, or on Low for 4 hours, or until fruit is bubbly.

6. Thirty minutes before end of cooking time, remove lid (don't let condensation from inside of lid drip on the crisp), so the topping can dry.

Serving suggestion:

Serve as is, topped with ice cream, or in a bowl with milk.

Apple Cranberry Crisp

Phyllis Good
Lancaster, PA

Makes 8–10 servings

Prep. Time: 20 minutes ❧ *Cooking Time: 4½–4¾ hours* ❧ *Ideal slow-cooker size: 4-qt.*

3 cups chopped apples, unpeeled

2 cups raw cranberries

⅓ cup granulated white sugar

Nonstick cooking spray or butter to grease slow-cooker crock

1½ cups old-fashioned or quick-cooking oats, uncooked

½ cup brown sugar

⅓ cup all-purpose flour

⅓ cup chopped pecans

1 stick (½ cup) butter, melted

Whipped cream, optional

1. Combine the apples, cranberries, and granulated white sugar in a greased slow-cooker crock. Mix thoroughly to blend everything well.

2. Cover. Cook on Low for 4 hours, or until the apples are as soft as you want.

3. While the apples and cranberries are cooking, in a good-sized bowl combine the oats, brown sugar, flour, pecans, and butter. Mix until the topping turns crumbly. Set it aside.

4. When the apples are finished cooking, scatter the topping over the hot fruit.

5. Continue cooking, uncovered, for 30 to 45 minutes, or until the topping is warm and beginning to brown around the edges. Serve warm with whipped cream if you wish.

Slow-Cooker Peach Crisp

Amanda Gross
Souderton, PA

Makes 6 servings

Prep. Time: 15 minutes ☙ *Cooking Time: 4–5 hours* ☙ *Ideal slow-cooker size: 6-qt.*

¼ cup biscuit baking mix

⅔ cup quick or rolled oats

1½ teaspoons ground cinnamon

¾ cup brown sugar

4 cups canned peaches, cut in quarters or slices, juice reserved

½ cup peach juice from jar

Nonstick cooking spray or butter to grease slow-cooker crock

1. Mix the biscuit mix, oats, cinnamon, and brown sugar in a bowl.

2. Place the peaches and juice in greased slow-cooker crock.

3. Add the oat mix. Stir gently once or twice so as not to break the peaches.

4. Cook on Low for 4 to 5 hours. Remove lid for the last 30 minutes of cooking.

Variation:

Use canned pears instead of peaches.

Peaches and Pudding Crisp

SLOW-COOKER

Phyllis Good
Lancaster, PA

Makes 8 servings

Prep. Time: 20 minutes ⚘ *Cooking Time: 3–4 hours* ⚘ *Ideal slow-cooker size: 5-qt.*

Nonstick cooking spray or butter to grease slow-cooker crock

5–6 cups peaches, fresh or canned

½ cup peach juice or syrup

2 small packages instant vanilla pudding, divided

½ cup brown sugar

Topping:

1 cup flour

1½ cups dry oatmeal, quick or rolled

½ cup brown sugar

8 tablespoons (1 stick) butter, melted

¾ teaspoon salt

2 teaspoons cinnamon

Reserved dry instant vanilla pudding

1. Grease interior of slow-cooker crock.

2. Combine the peaches, peach juice, 2 tablespoons dry pudding mix, and brown sugar in a good-sized mixing bowl. Set aside remaining dry pudding mix.

3. Place mixture in slow-cooker crock.

4. Combine all topping ingredients until well blended and crumbly. Sprinkle topping over the peach mixture.

5. Cover. Bake on High for 2½ to 3½ hours, or until firm in middle and bubbly around the edges.

6. Remove lid carefully, tilting it quickly away from yourself so that water from the inside of the lid doesn't drip on the crisp.

7. Continue baking for 30 more minutes so crisp dries out on top.

8. Remove crock from cooker and place on baking rack to cool. Serve when warm or at room temperature.

Tip:

I like the crisp to be crunchy, and it won't get brown on top in a slow cooker. So I like to run the finished dish under the broiler for just a minute or two until it's properly brown and crunchy. That, against the soft peaches—yum!

Summer Peach and Blackberry Crisp

Becky Lumetta
Romeo, MI

Makes 9 servings

Prep. Time: 15 minutes   Cooking/Baking Time: 40–45 minutes

Nonstick cooking spray

Topping:

¾ cup brown sugar

⅔ cup all-purpose flour

⅔ cup old-fashioned rolled oats

½ teaspoon ground nutmeg

1 teaspoon ground cinnamon

¼ teaspoon salt

½ cup cold unsalted butter, cut into small cubes

Filling:

4 cups sliced, ripe peaches (can use frozen, do not thaw)

1 pint blackberries

¼ cup all-purpose flour

¼ cup sugar

½ cup brown sugar

Zest and juice of 1 lemon

¼ teaspoon salt

½ teaspoon vanilla extract

1. Lightly spray an 8×8-inch square baking dish. Preheat oven to 375°F and position rack in middle of oven. Make topping.

2. For topping: Mix all the dry ingredients in a food processor. Add the butter cubes and pulse until mixture resembles coarse crumbs.

3. For filling: Mix the peaches and blackberries gently in a large bowl. Drizzle with the lemon juice.

4. Mix the flour, sugars, lemon zest, salt, and vanilla in a small bowl to blend. Sprinkle the mixture over the fruit and stir to coat. Pour into the prepared baking dish.

5. Sprinkle the topping evenly over the filling. Bake for 35 to 40 minutes, or until the filling is bubbly and the topping is golden brown.

Note:

This delicious crisp can be served warm or cooled. It is best with ice cream.

Nectarine Almond Crisp

Hope Comerford
Clinton Township, MI

Makes 8–9 servings

Prep. Time: 10 minutes & Cooking Time: 2 hours & Ideal slow-cooker size: 3- or 4-qt.

Nonstick cooking spray
5 nectarines, cored and sliced
¼ cup slivered almonds
1 teaspoon cinnamon
¼ teaspoon nutmeg
¼ teaspoon ginger
1 teaspoon vanilla extract

Crumble:
1 cup gluten-free oats
½ cup almond flour
½ cup slivered almonds
1 teaspoon cinnamon
¼ teaspoon ginger
½ teaspoon sea salt
2 tablespoons honey
2 tablespoons coconut oil, melted
2–3 tablespoons unsweetened
almond milk

1. Spray the slow-cooker crock with the nonstick cooking spray.

2. In the prepared crock, combine the nectarines, almonds, cinnamon, nutmeg, ginger, and vanilla.

3. In a medium bowl, combine all the crumble ingredients. If the mixture is too dry, add a bit more honey or almond milk. Pour the crumble over the top of the nectarine mixture.

4. Cover and cook on Low for 2 hours.

Apricot Crisp

SLOW-COOKER

Phyllis Good
Lancaster, PA

Makes 5 servings

Prep. Time: 20–30 minutes   ☘   Cooking Time: 3½–4 hours   ☘   Ideal slow-cooker size: 4-qt.

Nonstick cooking spray or butter to grease slow-cooker crock

2¼ lbs. fresh apricots

1¼ cups flour

¼ cup chopped walnuts or pecans

1¼ cups sugar

Pinch ground cloves

Pinch cardamom

1 teaspoon cinnamon

12 tablespoons (1½ sticks) butter

Variation:

Try these with canned apricots, too. But drain them well before using. Cut the sugar in half if the syrup is sweetened.

1. Grease the interior of the slow-cooker crock.

2. Cut the apricots in half, remove the stones, and place the fruit evenly into the prepared crock.

3. In a good-sized bowl, mix the flour, chopped walnuts, sugar, cloves, cardamom, and cinnamon until well blended.

4. Cut the butter into chunks. Using either your fingers, 2 knives, or a pastry cutter, work the butter into the dry ingredients.

5. When the mixture crumbly, scatter it over the apricot halves.

6. Cover. Bake on High for 3 to 3½ hours, or until fruit is tender.

7. Remove the lid carefully and quickly, tilting it away from yourself to prevent condensation on inside of lid from dripping onto crisp. Continue baking uncovered for another 30 minutes so crisp dries on top.

8. Remove the crock from the cooker and place it on a wire baking rack to cool. Serve crisp warm or at room temperature.

Old-Timey Raisin Crisp

SLOW-COOKER

Phyllis Good
Lancaster, PA

Makes 12 servings

Prep. Time: 20 minutes   ❧   Cooking Time: 2½–3½ hours
Standing Time: 1 hour   ❧   Ideal slow-cooker size: 5-qt.

Nonstick cooking spray or butter to grease slow-cooker crock

1 pound raisins

2 tablespoons cornstarch

½ cup sugar

1 cup water

2 tablespoons lemon juice

Crumbs:

1¾ cups flour

½ teaspoon baking soda

1 cup brown sugar

¼ teaspoon salt

1½ cups dry oats, quick or rolled

12 tablespoons (1½ sticks) butter

Tip:

Don't skip the lemon juice. It makes sure the crisp isn't supersweet. Add a little more if you'd like to really taste it.

1. Grease the interior of the slow cooker crock.

2. In a saucepan, combine the raisins, cornstarch, sugar, and water. Cook until slightly thickened, stirring continually.

3. Remove saucepan from the heat, stir in the lemon juice, and let cool for an hour.

4. Prepare the crumbs by combining the flour, baking soda, brown sugar, salt, and oats in a good-sized bowl until well mixed.

5. Cut the butter into chunks. Work it into the dry ingredients with your fingers, 2 knives, or a pastry cutter until fine crumbs form.

6. Divide the crumbs in half. Spread half the crumbs into the bottom of the slow-cooker crock. Press down to form crust.

7. Spoon the raisin mixture over the crumb crust.

8. Cover with remaining half of the crumbs.

9. Cover. Bake on High for 2 to 3 hours, or until firm in middle and bubbly around the edges.

10. Remove the lid carefully and quickly so drops of water from inside the lid don't drip on the crisp.

11. Continue baking 30 more minutes to allow the crisp to dry on top.

12. Remove the crock from the cooker and place it on a baking rack.

13. Cut into squares, or spoon out of crock, to serve when warm or at room temperature.

Rhubarb Crunch

Phyllis Good
Lancaster, PA

Makes 6–8 servings

Prep. Time: 30 minutes ⚜ *Cooking Time: 1½–2 hours* ⚜ *Ideal slow-cooker size: 3-qt.*

I cup flour, sifted (use ¼ cup whole wheat and ½ cup white if you wish)

¼ cup dry oats, quick or rolled

I cup brown sugar, packed

8 tablespoons butter (I stick), melted

I teaspoon cinnamon

I cup granulated white sugar

2 tablespoons cornstarch

I cup water

I teaspoon vanilla extract

2 cups diced rhubarb

1. In a good-sized bowl, stir the flour, oats, brown sugar, melted butter, and cinnamon until crumbly.

2. Set aside half the crumbs. Pat the remaining crumbs over the bottom of the slow-cooker crock.

3. Combine the granulated white sugar, cornstarch, water, and vanilla in a 2-qt. microwave-safe bowl, stirring until smooth.

4. Add the rhubarb to the water/sugar mixture. Microwave, covered, on High for 2 minutes. Stir. Cook for another minute, or until mixture becomes thick and clear, stirring frequently.

5. Pour the rhubarb sauce over the crumbs in crock.

6. Crumble the remaining crumbs over the top of the sauce.

7. Cover. Bake on High for 1 hour.

8. Uncover. (Make sure the lid doesn't drip water on top of crunch when removing it.) Bake on High an additional 30 to 60 minutes, or until crunch is crunchy on top.

9. Remove the crock from the cooker. Allow crunch to cool until it's warm or room temperature before digging in.

Munchy Rhubary Crunch

SLOW-COOKER

Jane Geigley
Lancaster, PA

Makes 3 servings

Prep. Time: 30 minutes ❧ *Cooking Time: 2–3 hours* ❧ *Ideal slow-cooker size: 3-qt.*

1 cup sifted flour

¾ cup rolled oats

1 cup brown sugar

8 tablespoons butter, melted

1 teaspoon cinnamon

Nonstick cooking spray or butter to grease slow-cooker crock

4 cups diced rhubarb

1 cup sugar

2 tablespoons cornstarch

1 cup water

1 teaspoon vanilla extract

1. Mix the flour, oats, brown sugar, butter, and cinnamon to make crumbs.

2. Grease slow-cooker crock and press half of the crumbs into the prepared crock.

3. Layer the rhubarb over the top of the crumbs.

4. Mix the sugar, cornstarch, water, and vanilla in a small pan and cook until thick and clear (constantly stirring).

5. Pour over the sugar mixture over the rhubarb.

6. Top with the remaining crumbs.

7. Cover and cook on High for 2 to 3 hours.

Strawberry Rhubarb Crisp

SLOW-COOKER

Hope Comerford
Clinton Township, MI

Makes 6–8 servings

Prep. Time: 30 minutes ⚘ *Cooking Time: 2–3 hours* ⚘ *Ideal slow-cooker size: 2½-qt.*

Nonstick cooking spray

Filling:

1 pound strawberries, quartered if medium or large

3 rhubarb stalks, halved and sliced

½ cup sugar

2 tablespoons flour

2 teaspoons vanilla extract

Crisp:

½ cup sugar

2 tablespoons flour

½ teaspoon cinnamon

Pinch salt

3 tablespoons unsalted butter, cold and sliced

½ cup old-fashioned oats

2 tablespoons chopped pecans

2 tablespoons chopped almonds

1. Spray the slow-cooker crock with nonstick cooking spray.

2. Place the strawberries and rhubarb into the prepared slow-cooker crock.

3. In a bowl, mix the sugar, flour, and vanilla. Pour this over the strawberries and rhubarb in the slow-cooker crock and stir to coat evenly.

4. In another bowl, start on the crisp. Mix the sugar, flour, cinnamon, and salt. Cut the butter in with a pastry cutter.

5. Stir in the oats, pecans, and almonds. Pour this mixture over the contents of the slow-cooker crock.

6. Cover and cook on Low for 2 to 3 hours.

7. During the last half hour of cooking, remove the lid to help the crisp thicken.

Strawberry Crisp

SLOW-COOKER

Phyllis Good
Lancaster, PA

Makes 6 servings

Prep. Time: 30 minutes ⚶ Cooking Time: 2½–3½ hours ⚶ Ideal slow-cooker size: 4-qt.

Nonstick cooking spray or butter to grease slow-cooker crock

1 cup dry oats, quick or rolled

1 cup flour

1 cup brown sugar, packed

8 tablespoons (1 stick) butter

4 cups sliced fresh strawberries

⅓ cup sugar, or less

1. Grease interior of slow-cooker crock.

2. In a good-sized bowl, combine oats, flour, and brown sugar. Cut the butter into chunks and work it into the dry ingredients with your fingers, 2 knives, or a pastry cutter until crumbly.

3. In a separate bowl, gently mix the sliced strawberries and sugar.

4. Divide the crumbs in half. Place half the crumbs into the bottom of the prepared slow-cooker crock. Press down to form crust.

5. Spoon the strawberries evenly over the crust.

6. Scatter the remaining half of the crumbs over the strawberries.

7. Cover. Bake on High for 2 to 3 hours, or until firm in the center and bubbly around the edges.

8. Remove the lid carefully with a swift swoop away from yourself to keep condensation on the inside of the lid from dripping onto crisp. Continue baking on High for another 30 minutes to allow the crisp to dry on top.

9. Remove the crock from the cooker and place it on a wire baking rack to cool. Serve warm or at room temperature.

Strawberry Mint Crisp

Hope Comerford
Clinton Township, MI

Makes 4 servings

Prep. Time: 20 minutes & Cooking Time: 2 hours & Ideal slow-cooker size: 2- or 3-qt.

Nonstick cooking spray

2½–3 cups sliced strawberries

1 teaspoon cinnamon

½ teaspoon mint extract

1 teaspoon vanilla extract

3 tablespoons fresh chopped mint

Crumble:

½ cup gluten-free oats

¼ cup gluten-free oat flour

½ teaspoon cinnamon

¼ teaspoon salt

1 tablespoon honey

1 tablespoon coconut oil, melted

1–2 tablespoons unsweetened almond
or coconut milk

1. Spray the slow-cooker crock with nonstick cooking spray.

2. In the prepared crock, combine the strawberries, cinnamon, mint extract, vanilla, and fresh chopped mint.

3. In a bowl, combine all the crumble ingredients. If it's too dry, add a bit more honey or milk of your choice. Pour this mixture into the prepared slow-cooker crock.

4. Cover and cook on Low for 2 hours.

Blueberry Crisp

SLOW-COOKER

Phyllis Good
Lancaster, PA

Makes 6–8 servings

Prep. Time: 15–20 minutes ⚘ *Cooking Time: 2 hours* ⚘ *Ideal slow-cooker size: 4-qt.*

½ cup brown sugar

¾ cup dry rolled oats

½ cup whole wheat flour or all-purpose flour

½ teaspoon cinnamon

Dash salt

6 tablespoons butter, at room temperature

4 cups blueberries, fresh or frozen

2–4 tablespoons sugar, depending on how sweet you like things

2 tablespoons instant tapioca

2 tablespoons lemon juice

½ teaspoon lemon zest

Nonstick cooking spray or butter

1. In a large bowl, combine the brown sugar, oats, flour, cinnamon, and salt. Cut in the butter using a pastry cutter or two knives to make crumbs. Set aside.

2. In a separate bowl, stir together the blueberries, sugar, tapioca, lemon juice, and lemon zest.

3. Grease the slow-cooker crock. Spoon the blueberry mixture into the prepared slow-cooker crock. Sprinkle the crumbs over the blueberries.

4. Cover and cook on High for 1½ hours. Remove the lid and cook for an additional 30 minutes on High.

Blueberry Crinkle

Phyllis Good
Lancaster, PA

Makes 6–8 servings

Prep. Time: 15–20 minutes ⚭ *Baking Time: 20 minutes*

½ cup brown sugar

¾ cup dry quick oats

½ cup white or whole wheat flour

½ teaspoon cinnamon

Dash salt

6 tablespoons butter, at room temperature

4 cups blueberries, fresh or frozen

2 tablespoons sugar

2 tablespoons instant tapioca

2 tablespoons lemon juice

½ teaspoon lemon zest

Nonstick cooking spray or butter to grease baking dish

1. In a large bowl, combine the brown sugar, oats, flour, cinnamon, and salt. Cut in the butter to make crumbs. Set aside.

2. In a separate bowl, stir together the blueberries, sugar, tapioca, lemon juice, and lemon zest.

3. Grease an 8×8-inch baking dish. Spoon the blueberry mixture into the prepared baking dish and sprinkle the crumbs over the blueberries.

4. Bake at 375°F for 20 minutes.

Mixed Fruit Crisp Delight

OVEN

Willard Swartley
Elkhart, IN

Makes 6–8 servings

Prep. Time: 30 minutes ⚮ *Baking Time: 40 minutes*

2 cups sour cherries, peaches or rhubarb

3 cups mulberries or blackberries, or 2 cups strawberries

½–¾ cup sugar, according to your taste preference

¾ cup water

3 tablespoons cornstarch or minute tapioca

Nonstick cooking spray or butter to grease baking dish

1¾ cups quick oats

1 cup flour

¾ cup brown sugar

½ teaspoon baking soda

3 tablespoons butter, softened

½ cup chopped walnuts

1. Pit the sour cherries. Cut up chosen fruits.

2. In a saucepan over low heat, cook the chosen fruits, sugar, water, and cornstarch until thickened.

3. Grease a 2-qt. baking dish. Pour the fruit mixture into the prepared baking dish.

4. Mix the oats, flour, brown sugar, baking soda, butter, and walnuts. Sprinkle the dry mixture over the top of the fruit mixture in the baking dish.

5. Bake at 350°F for 30 minutes, or until top is slightly browned and edges are bubbling.

Cherry Crisp

Veronica Marshall-Varela
Chandler, AZ

Makes 8 servings

Prep. Time: 15 minutes ✃ Baking Time: 30 minutes

21-ounce can cherry pie filling

16-ounce bag frozen pitted cherries, thawed

Nonstick cooking spray or butter to grease baking dish

Topping:

1 stick (½ cup) butter

1 cup rolled oats

1 cup brown sugar, packed

½ teaspoon cinnamon

¾ cup coarsely chopped walnuts or pecans

½ cup coconut

Vanilla ice cream or whipped cream

1. Mix the pie filling and cherries and place in greased 8×8-inch baking dish.

2. To make topping, place the butter in a medium-sized microwaveable bowl. Microwave in 20-second increments, checking until butter is completely melted.

3. Add the oats, brown sugar, cinnamon, walnuts, and coconut. Stir.

4. Sprinkle the topping over cherry filling.

5. Bake for 30 minutes at 375°F or until bubbly around the edges. Serve warm with vanilla ice cream or whipped cream.

Blueberry Raspberry Crunch

Darla Sathre
Baxter, MN

Makes 12 servings

Prep. Time: 15 minutes ⚬ *Cooking/Baking Time: 25–30 minutes*

21-ounce can blueberry pie filling

21-ounce can raspberry pie filling

Nonstick cooking spray or butter to grease baking dish

18¼-ounce package white cake mix

¼ cup chopped walnuts

1 stick (½ cup) butter, melted

1. Combine the pie fillings in a lightly greased 9×13-inch baking dish.

2. In a mixing bowl, combine the dry cake mix, walnuts, and butter. Sprinkle the mixture over the pie filling.

3. Bake at 375°F for 25 to 30 minutes, or until golden brown. Serve warm or cold.

Crumbles

Apple Peanut Crumble

SLOW-
COOKER

Phyllis Attig
Reynolds, IL

Joan Becker
Dodge City, KS

Pam Hochstedler
Kalona, IA

Makes 4–5 servings

Prep. Time: 10 minutes ❧ *Cooking Time: 5–6 hours* ❧ *Ideal slow-cooker size: 4-qt.*

4–5 cooking apples, peeled and sliced
⅔ cup packed brown sugar
½ cup flour
½ cup quick-cooking dry oats
½ teaspoon cinnamon
¼–½ teaspoon nutmeg
⅓ cup butter, softened
2 tablespoons peanut butter

1. Place the apple slices in the slow-cooker crock.

2. Combine the brown sugar, flour, oats, cinnamon, and nutmeg.

3. Cut in the butter and peanut butter. Sprinkle the mixture over the apples.

4. Cover the slow cooker and cook on Low for 5 to 6 hours.

Serving suggestion:

Serve warm or cold, plain or with ice cream or whipped cream.

Harvest Goodie

SLOW-COOKER

MarJanita Geigley
Lancaster, PA

Makes 5–6 servings

Prep. Time: 30 minutes ⚜ *Cooking Time: 2–4 hours* ⚜ *Ideal slow-cooker size: 4-qt.*

Nonstick cooking spray or butter to grease slow-cooker crock

2 cups sliced apples

2 cups sliced peaches

¾ cup brown sugar

½ cup flour

½ cup oats

⅓ cup softened butter

¾ teaspoon cinnamon

¾ teaspoon nutmeg

1. Spray or grease slow-cooker crock.

2. In the prepared slow-cooker crock, mix the apples and peaches.

3. In a mixing bowl, combine the other ingredients and pour them over the top of the fruit in the slow-cooker crock.

4. Cook on Low for 2 to 4 hours.

Serving suggestion:

Serve warm and with vanilla-bean ice cream or a cold glass of milk.

Peach Crumble

OVEN

Nathan LeBeau
Rapid City, SD

Makes 6–8 servings

Prep. Time: 10 minutes   *Baking Time: 20–30 minutes*

¾ cup brown sugar

4 cups peeled, sliced fresh peaches

Nonstick cooking spray or butter to grease baking dish

⅓ cup (5⅓ tablespoons) butter, softened

¾ teaspoon nutmeg

¾ teaspoon cinnamon

1 cup graham cracker crumbs

1. Mix the brown sugar and peaches.

2. Grease an 8×8-inch baking dish. Pour peach mixture into prepared dish.

3. Combine the butter, nutmeg, cinnamon, and graham crackers. Mix well.

4. Sprinkle the mixture over the top of the peaches.

5. Bake at 375°F for 20 to 30 minutes until bubbling.

Variation:

Use apples instead of peaches.

Quick Yummy Peaches

Willard E. Roth
Elkhart, IN

Makes 8 servings

Prep. Time: 20 minutes ⚜ *Cooking Time: 20 minutes* ⚜ *Setting: Manual*
Pressure: High ⚜ *Release: Natural and Manual* ⚜ *Cooling Time: 20–30 minutes*

⅓ cup buttermilk baking mix

⅔ cup dry quick oats

¼ cup brown sugar

Brown sugar substitute to equal
2 tablespoons sugar

1 teaspoon cinnamon

4 cups sliced peaches, canned or fresh

½ cup peach juice or water

1 cup water

1. Mix the baking mix, oats, brown sugar, brown sugar substitute, and cinnamon. Mix in the peaches and peach juice.

2. Pour mixture into a 1.6-qt. baking dish. Cover with foil.

3. Place the trivet into your Instant Pot and pour in the water. Place a foil sling on top of the trivet, then place the baking dish on top.

4. Secure the lid and make sure lid is set to sealing. Press Manual and set for 10 minutes.

5. When cook time is up, let the pressure release naturally for 10 minutes, then release any remaining pressure manually. Carefully remove the baking dish by using hot pads to lift the foil sling. Uncover and let cool for about 20 to 30 minutes.

Deep Dish Fruity Delight

SLOW-COOKER

Phyllis Good
Lancaster, PA

Makes 12–15 servings

Prep. Time: 15 minutes ⚬ *Cooking Time: 3½–4 hours* ⚬ *Ideal slow-cooker size: 5- or 6-qt.*

Nonstick cooking spray or butter to grease slow-cooker crock

20-ounce can crushed pineapple, drained

21-ounce can cherry, apple, or blueberry pie filling

18¼-ounce box yellow cake or angel food cake mix

8 tablespoons (1 stick) butter, melted

½–1 cup chopped nuts

1. Grease interior of slow-cooker crock.

2. Spread the drained pineapple over the bottom of the prepared crock.

3. Spoon the pie filling evenly over the pineapple.

4. Sprinkle the dry cake mix over the pie filling.

5. Drizzle the melted butter over the dry cake mix.

6. Sprinkle with the nuts.

7. Cover. Bake on High 3½–4 hours, or until tester inserted into center of cobbler comes out clean.

8. Uncover, being careful not to let water from inside of lid drip on cobbler. Remove crock from cooker and place on wire baking rack to cool.

9. When warm or room temperature, slice or spoon out to serve.

Variation:

Add 1 cup flaked or grated coconut to step 6 if you wish.

Jumbleberry Crumble

Joanna Harrison
Lafayette, CO

Makes 6–8 servings

Prep. Time: 20 minutes & Baking Time: 50 minutes

3 cups strawberries

1 ½ cups blueberries

1 ½ cups raspberries

3 tablespoons Minute Tapioca

⅔ cup sugar

Nonstick cooking spray or butter to grease baking dish

½ cup flour

½ cup quick oats

½ cup brown sugar, packed

1 teaspoon cinnamon

⅓ cup (5 tablespoons) butter, melted

1. In a large bowl, combine the berries, tapioca, and sugar.

2. Grease an 11x7-inch baking dish and pour the berry mixture into the prepared dish. Let stand 15 minutes.

3. Combine the flour, oats, brown sugar, and cinnamon in small bowl.

4. Stir in the melted butter.

5. Sprinkle the topping over the berry mixture.

6. Bake at 350°F for 45 to 50 minutes or until the filling is bubbly and the topping is golden brown. Serve warm.

Tip:

I've used fresh or frozen berries depending on the season. This is yummy with vanilla ice cream.

Chocolate Cherry Cheesecake Crumble

SLOW-COOKER

Sue Hamilton
Benson, AZ

Makes 4 servings

Prep. Time: 10 minutes   ⚶   *Cooking Time: 1½ hours*   ⚶   *Ideal slow-cooker size: 2-qt.*

Nonstick cooking spray

15-ounce can of dark sweet cherries with juice

3.4-ounce box of cheesecake instant pudding mix

12 double-stuff chocolate sandwich cookies, broken (I just use my hands)

4 tablespoons butter, melted

1. Spray the slow-cooker crock with nonstick cooking spray.

2. Pour the cherries into the prepared crock. Add 14 tablespoons of the instant pudding and stir it in.

3. In a bowl, combine the broken cookies and the butter. Stir until well mixed.

4. Add the rest of the dry pudding mix to the cookie mixture. Spoon the mixture evenly on top of the fruit.

5. Cover and cook on High for 1½ hours.

Serving suggestion:

Serve warm with whipped cream.

Cherry Crumble

OVEN

Jeanne Allen
Rye, CO

Makes 6 servings

Prep. Time: 15–30 minutes ⚜ *Cooking/Baking Time: 40–45 minutes*

10⅔ tablespoons (⅔ cup) butter, softened

¾ cup brown, or granulated, sugar

1½ cups flour

1 cup dry quick oats

1 can cherry pie filling, or flavor of your choice

Extra butter, optional

Whipped topping or cream, optional

1. In a large mixing bowl, mix all the ingredients except the cherry pie filling, extra butter, and whipped topping.

2. Reserve 1½ cups of the crumbs for topping.

3. Line an ungreased 9×9-inch baking dish with the remaining crumbs.

4. Spoon the cherry pie filling over the top of the crumbs.

5. Top with the reserved crumbs.

6. Dot with the extra butter, if you wish.

7. Bake at 350°F for 40 to 45 minutes, or until golden brown.

8. Serve warm or cold, with the whipped topping, if you wish.

Cobblers

Apple Cobbler

Kendra Dreps
Liberty, PA

Makes 8 servings

Prep. Time: 25 minutes   ♣   Cooking Time: 2–4 hours   ♣   Ideal slow-cooker size: 4–6 qt.

Nonstick cooking spray
7–8 apples, peeled and sliced
2½ cups sugar, divided
¾ teaspoon cinnamon, divided
2 cups flour
2 teaspoons baking powder
¾ teaspoon salt
2 eggs
⅔ cup butter, melted

1. Spray the slow-cooker crock with nonstick cooking spray.

2. Combine the apples, ½ cup sugar, and ½ teaspoon cinnamon. Place in prepared slow cooker.

3. Combine ¼ teaspoon cinnamon with the flour, baking powder, salt, and eggs. Pour the mixture evenly on top of the apples.

4. Pour the melted butter over all.

5. Cover and cook on Low for 2 to 4 hours, until the apples are tender and the top is baked.

Tip:

Serve warm with vanilla ice cream.

Texas Peach Cobbler

OVEN

Edna Good
Richland Center, WI

Makes 9 servings

Prep. Time: 20 minutes & Baking Time: 50 minutes

6 tablespoons butter

1 ¼ cups all-purpose flour

¾ cup, plus 2 tablespoons, sugar, divided

2 teaspoons baking powder

⅛ teaspoon salt

Dash cinnamon

1 teaspoon vanilla extract, divided

1 cup milk

4 cups peaches, peeled and sliced

1 teaspoon lemon juice

1. Turn oven on to 350°F. Place the butter in an 8×8-inch baking dish. Place the dish in the oven to melt the butter.

2. In mixing bowl, combine the flour, ¾ cup sugar, baking powder, salt, cinnamon, ½ teaspoon vanilla, and milk. Stir just until combined.

3. Spoon the batter over the melted butter. Do not mix!

4. In a bowl, combine the peaches, 1 tablespoon sugar, the lemon juice, and remaining ½ teaspoon vanilla.

5. Spoon the peach mixture over the batter, gently pressing the peaches into the batter.

6. Bake at 350°F for 40 minutes.

7. Sprinkle with the remaining 1 tablespoon sugar and bake for 10 minutes longer.

Apple Gingerbread Cobbler

OVEN

Esther H. Becker
Gordonville, PA

Makes 12–15 servings

Prep. Time: 15 minutes ⚭ Cooking/Baking Time: 35 minutes

4 tablespoons (½ stick) butter

2 (21-ounce) cans apple pie filling

15-ounce box gingerbread mix

1. Melt the butter in a large saucepan.

2. Stir in the apple pie filling. Remove the saucepan from the heat.

3. Spread the filling mixture into a 9x13-inch cake pan.

4. Make the gingerbread batter according to the directions on the box.

5. Pour the gingerbread batter on top of the apple pie filling.

6. Bake at 350°F for 35 minutes, or until a toothpick inserted in the middle of the cake comes out clean.

Peach Cobbler

SLOW-COOKER

Phyllis Good
Lancaster, PA

Makes 8 servings

Prep. Time: 20 minutes ☙ Cooking Time: 3–4 hours ☙ Ideal slow-cooker size: 5-qt.

Nonstick cooking spray

3–4 cups sliced peaches

⅓ cup and ½ cup granulated white sugar, divided

¼ cup brown sugar

Dash nutmeg

Dash cinnamon

8 tablespoons (1 stick) butter

¾ cup flour

2 teaspoons baking powder

¾ cup milk

1. Spray the slow-cooker crock with nonstick cooking spray.

2. Mix in a good-sized bowl the peaches, ⅓ cup granulated white sugar, brown sugar, nutmeg, and cinnamon. Set aside to macerate.

3. Place the butter in the slow-cooker crock turned on High, and let it melt there.

4. In a bowl, stir together ½ cup granulated white sugar and the flour, baking powder, and milk until smooth.

5. When the butter is melted, make sure it covers the bottom of the slow-cooker crock. Spoon the batter evenly over the butter in the crock, but don't stir.

6. Spoon the sugared peaches over the batter.

7. Cover. Bake on High for 3 to 4 hours, or until firm in the middle and bubbly around the edges.

8. Uncover carefully so condensation from the inside of the lid doesn't drip on the cobbler. Remove the crock from the cooker.

Variations:

Love this in the summertime! But it's also good with canned or frozen peaches. Drain canned peaches or thaw frozen ones before adding them to the crock. The cobbler won't firm up well if you add that extra moisture.

Serving suggestion:

Serve while warm with milk or ice cream.

Plum Cobbler

Phyllis Good
Lancaster, PA

Makes 9 servings

Prep. Time: 10–15 minutes ⚘ *Cooking Time: 1½–1¾ hours* ⚘ *Ideal slow-cooker size: 4-qt.*

¼ cup (half stick) butter, softened

¼ cup sugar

2 eggs

1 teaspoon lemon zest

1 cup all-purpose flour

1 teaspoon baking powder

¼ cup milk

Nonstick cooking spray or butter to grease slow-cooker crock

2½ cups sliced fresh plums, unpeeled (about 4 medium-sized ones)

2 teaspoons cinnamon

½ cup brown sugar

1. In a mixing bowl, cream the butter and sugar together.

2. Beat in the eggs and lemon zest.

3. In a separate bowl, combine the flour and baking powder.

4. Stir the flour mixture into the creamed ingredients. Add the milk, mixing well.

5. Lightly grease the slow-cooker crock and pour the batter into the prepared crock.

6. Arrange the plums on top of the batter.

7. In a small bowl, stir together the cinnamon and brown sugar. Sprinkle the mixture over the plums.

8. Cover and cook on High for 1 to 1¼ hours, until cobbler is nearly set in the middle and plums are juicy. Remove the lid and cook for another 30 minutes on High.

Cherry Cobbler

Michele Ruvola
Selden, NY

Makes 6–8 servings

Prep Time: 5 minutes   Cooking Time: 2½–5½ hours   Ideal slow-cooker size: 3-qt.

Nonstick cooking spray
16-ounce can cherry pie filling
1¾ cups dry cake mix of your choice
1 egg
3 tablespoons evaporated milk
½ teaspoon cinnamon

1. Lightly spray the slow-cooker crock with nonstick cooking spray.

2. Place pie filling in prepared slow-cooker crock and cook on High for 30 minutes.

3. Meanwhile, mix the remaining ingredients in a bowl until crumbly. Spoon onto the hot pie filling.

4. Cover and cook on Low for 2 to 5 hours, or until a toothpick inserted into center of topping comes out dry.

5. Serve warm or cooled.

Cobbler with Fresh Cherries

Phyllis Good
Lancaster, PA

Makes 6 servings

Prep. Time: 20 minutes   Cooking Time: 2½–3½ hours
Standing Time: 1 hour   Ideal slow-cooker size: 4-qt.

Nonstick cooking spray or butter to grease slow-cooker crock

4 cups (about 2 lbs.) pitted fresh cherries, sweet or sour

⅓–¾ cup sugar, depending on how sweet the cherries are

1 tablespoon instant tapioca

⅓ cup water

1 tablespoon butter

Cobbler Batter:

8 tablespoons (1 stick) butter

1¼ cups flour

1 cup sugar

2 tablespoons baking powder

½ teaspoon salt

1 cup milk

Variation:

You can use canned or frozen cherries for this. If canned, cut the sugar back and use the juice instead of the water that's called for. I love sour cherries here because of the tart–sweet combination!

1. Grease interior of slow-cooker crock.

2. In a good-sized saucepan, combine the pitted cherries, the lesser amount of sugar, the tapioca, and water.

3. Let stand for an hour, stirring now and then. Test the mixture to see if it's the sweetness you like. Now's the time to add more sugar if you want.

4. Cook over medium heat until boiling, stirring continually to prevent sticking and scorching. Simmer for 5 to 10 minutes, stirring constantly.

5. Remove from the heat. Stir in 1 tablespoon butter.

6. To make the batter, cut up the stick of butter into the slow-cooker crock. Turn cooker to High so butter melts.

7. Meanwhile, combine the flour, sugar, baking powder, and salt in a good-sized bowl. When well mixed, stir in milk until batter is smooth.

8. Drop batter by spoonfuls evenly over melted butter in crock. Do not stir.

9. Spoon the thickened cherry mixture over the batter. Do not stir.

10. Cover. Cook on High for 2 to 3 hours, or until firm in middle and bubbly around edges.

11. Remove the lid carefully and swiftly so no drops of water from the lid drip onto the cobbler. Continue baking on High for 30 more minutes so cobbler becomes drier on top.

12. Remove the crock from the cooker and place on baking rack to cool. When warm or room temperature, serve.

Holiday Cherry Cobbler

SLOW-COOKER

Colleen Heatwole
Burton, MI

Makes 5–6 servings

Prep. Time: 15 minutes ⚬ *Cooking Time: 2½–3½ hours* ⚬ *Ideal slow-cooker size: 4-qt.*

Nonstick cooking spray

16-ounce can cherry filling (light or regular)

1 package cake mix for 1 layer white, or yellow, cake

1 egg

3 tablespoons evaporated milk

½ teaspoon cinnamon

½ cup walnuts, chopped

1. Spray slow-cooker crock with nonstick cooking spray.

2. Spread the pie filling in the bottom of prepared slow-cooker crock.

3. Cover. Cook on High for 30 minutes.

4. In a medium-sized mixing bowl, mix the cake mix, egg, evaporated milk, cinnamon, and walnuts.

5. Spoon the mixture over the hot pie filling. Do not stir.

6. Cover. Cook on Low for 2 to 3 hours, or until toothpick inserted in cake layer comes out clean.

Edy's Easy Cherry Cobbler

OVEN

Carolyn Spohn
Shawnee, KS

Makes 4–6 servings

Prep. Time: 15 minutes ⚜ *Cooking/Baking Time: 25–30 minutes*

15-ounce can red tart cherries
1 cup sugar, divided
1 cup buttermilk baking mix
½ cup milk
Nonstick cooking spray

1. Drain the juice from the cherries into a glass measuring cup. Add ½ cup sugar and heat juice and sugar mixture in microwave until sugar is dissolved.

2. In a small mixing bowl, combine the baking mix with the remaining ½ cup sugar and ½ cup milk. Mix until all ingredients are moistened.

3. Spray a 9×9-inch baking dish with nonstick cooking spray. Spread the biscuit mixture in the bottom of the prepared baking dish.

4. Spread cherries evenly over this.

5. Carefully pour the juice and sugar mixture over the top of the cherries.

6. Bake at 350°F for 25 to 30 minutes, or until lightly browned. The cobbler is finished when a toothpick inserted into the center of the cake comes out clean. (The crust will rise to the top, and the cherries and their syrup will be underneath.)

Blackberry Cobbler

Virginia R. Bender
Dover, DE

Makes 6 servings

Prep. Time: 15 minutes ⚭ *Cooking/Baking Time: 40 minutes*

½ cup sugar
1 cup flour
½ cup milk
1 teaspoon baking powder
Nonstick cooking spray or butter to grease baking dish
2 cups blackberries

1. In a medium-sized mixing bowl, combine the sugar, flour, milk, and baking powder until well blended.

2. Lightly grease a 9×9-inch baking dish and pour the mixture into the prepared baking dish.

3. Spoon the fresh or frozen blackberries over the top.

4. Bake at 350°F for 40 minutes, or until a toothpick inserted in center comes out clean. The crust will rise to the top.

5. Serve warm.

Sour Cherry Cobbler

SLOW-COOKER

Margaret W. High
Lancaster, PA

Makes 6–8 servings

Prep. Time: 20 minutes   Cooking Time: 2 hours   Ideal slow-cooker size: 6-qt.

½ cup whole wheat flour

¾ cup all-purpose flour, divided

1 tablespoon sugar, plus ⅔ cup sugar, divided

1 teaspoon baking powder

¼ teaspoon salt

¼ teaspoon ground cinnamon

¼ teaspoon almond extract

1 egg

¼ cup milk

2 tablespoons melted butter

Nonstick cooking spray or butter to grease slow-cooker crock

4 cups pitted sour cherries, thawed and drained if frozen

1. In a mixing bowl, combine the whole wheat flour and ½ cup all-purpose flour. Mix in 1 tablespoon sugar and the baking powder, salt, and cinnamon.

2. Separately, combine the almond extract, egg, milk, and butter. Stir into dry ingredients just until moistened.

3. Grease the slow-cooker crock with the nonstick cooking spray. Spread the batter in the bottom of the prepared slow-cooker crock.

4. Separately, mix remaining ¼ cup flour with ⅔ cup sugar. Add the cherries. Sprinkle the cherry mixture evenly over the batter in the slow-cooker crock.

5. Cover and cook on High for 2 hours or until the cobbler is lightly browned at edges and the juice is bubbling from the cherries.

Variations:

1. Use blueberries instead of sour cherries.

2. Reduce sugar to 1/2 cup and use vanilla extract instead of almond.

Tip:

Cobblers are wonderful served warm with vanilla ice cream, whipped cream, or custard sauce.

No-Sugar-Added Cherry Cobbler

Janie Steele
Moore, OK

Makes 4 servings

Prep. Time: 20 minutes ✢ Cooking Time: 1–2 hours ✢ Ideal slow-cooker size: 2-qt.

Nonstick cooking spray or butter to grease slow-cooker crock

20-ounce can no-sugar-added cherry pie filling (can use other flavors)

1 cup flour

¼ cup melted butter

½ cup skim milk

1½ teaspoons baking powder

½ teaspoon almond extract

¼ teaspoon salt

Ice cream or whipped topping, optional

1. Grease slow-cooker crock.

2. Combine all the ingredients except ice cream or whipped topping in the prepared slow-cooker crock and mix until smooth.

3. Cover and cook for 1 to 2 hours, or until heated through.

4. Serve with ice cream or whipped topping, if desired.

Cherry Berry Cobbler

OVEN

Carol DiNuzzo
Latham, NY

Makes 6 servings

Prep. Time: 10 minutes ⚓ *Baking Time: 30 minutes*

21-ounce can cherry pie filling

10-ounce package frozen red raspberries, thawed and drained

1 teaspoon lemon juice

Nonstick cooking spray or butter to grease casserole dish

½ cup flour

¼ cup sugar

⅛ teaspoon salt

½ stick (1 tablespoons) butter

1. Preheat the oven to 350°F.

2. In a saucepan, combine pie filling, raspberries, and lemon juice. Bring to a boil over medium heat. Turn into a greased 1-qt. casserole dish.

3. In a bowl, mix together flour, sugar, and salt. Cut in butter until crumbly. Sprinkle over fruit.

4. Bake for 35 to 45 minutes, or until topping is lightly browned.

Serving suggestion:

Serve warm (not hot), alone or over ice cream.

Strawberry Cobbler

SLOW-COOKER

Karrie Molina
Freeland, MI

Makes 4 servings

Prep. Time: 10 min. ⚘ *Cooking Time: 1½–4 hours* ⚘ *Ideal slow-cooker size: 2-qt.*

½ of a 21-ounce can of strawberry pie filling (or cherry if you prefer)

½ of a box yellow cake mix

4 tablespoons butter, melted

1. Place the pie filling at the bottom of the slow-cooker crock.

2. In a separate bowl, combine the cake mix and butter.

3. Sprinkle the cake-mix-and-butter mixture over the pie filling. (Do not mix.)

4. Cover and cook on Low for 3 to 4 hours, or on High for 1½ to 2 hours.

Serving suggestion:

You can place ice cream alongside or whipped topping on individual servings.

Black and Blue Cobbler

Renee Shirk
Mount Joy, PA

Makes 6 servings

Prep. Time: 20 minutes ❧ *Cooking Time: 2–2½ hours* ❧ *Ideal slow-cooker size: 5-qt.*

1 cup almond flour

36 packets stevia, divided

1 teaspoon Low-Carb Baking Powder (see recipe on pg. 194)

¼ teaspoon salt

¼ teaspoon cinnamon

¼ teaspoon nutmeg

2 eggs, beaten

2 tablespoons whole milk

2 tablespoons coconut oil, melted

Nonstick cooking spray or butter to grease slow-cooker crock

2 cups fresh, or frozen, blueberries

2 cups fresh, or frozen, blackberries

¾ cup water

1 teaspoon grated orange peel

1. Combine the almond flour, 18 packets stevia, baking powder, salt, cinnamon, and nutmeg.

2. Combine the eggs, milk, and oil. Stir into dry ingredients until moistened.

3. Lightly grease the slow-cooker crock and spread the batter evenly over the bottom of the prepared slow-cooker crock.

4. In a saucepan, combine the berries, water, orange peel, and remaining 18 packets stevia. Bring to a boil. Remove from the heat and pour the berry mixture over the batter. Cover.

5. Cook on High for 2 to 2½ hours, or until toothpick inserted into the batter comes out clean. Turn off cooker.

6. Uncover and let stand for 30 minutes before serving.

Note:

This recipe is keto-friendly!

Berry Cobbler

OVEN

Eileen Eash
Carlsbad, NM

June S. Groff
Denver, PA

Sharon Wantland
Menomonee Falls, WI

Makes 10 servings

Prep. Time: 30 minutes ⚜ *Baking Time: 60–70 minutes*

8 cups sliced fresh, or frozen, mixed berries (raspberries, blackberries, strawberries)

8 tablespoons (1 stick) butter, softened

4½ tablespoons granulated stevia

1 cup almond flour

¼ teaspoon cinnamon mixed with ¼ teaspoon granulated stevia

1. Place the berries in an ungreased 9×13-inch baking dish.

2. In a medium-sized mixing bowl, cream the butter and stevia together, either with a spoon or an electric mixer.

3. Add the almond flour and mix well. Sprinkle the mixture over the berries.

4. Top with the cinnamon-stevia mix.

5. Bake at 325°F for 60 to 70 minutes, or until top is golden brown.

Serving suggestion:

Serve warm with milk or keto ice cream, if you wish.

Note:

This recipe is keto-friendly!

Fresh Berry Cobbler

OVEN

Abbie Christie
Berkeley Heights, NJ

Makes 8 servings (4½×2¼-inch rectangle each)

Prep. Time: 10 minutes ♣ *Baking Time: 45–50 minutes*

Nonstick cooking spray or butter to grease baking dish

1 tablespoon butter

3 tablespoons coconut oil, melted

1 cup almond flour

1 cup whole milk

½ cup Splenda Sugar Blend

2 teaspoons Low-Carb Baking Powder (recipe on pg. 194)

Dash salt

3–4 cups fresh berries

1. Preheat oven to 350°F.

2. Grease a 9×9-inch baking dish. Melt butter in the prepared baking dish.

3. Add all other ingredients except the berries. Stir well.

4. Arrange the fruit on top of the batter.

5. Bake for 45 to 50 minutes, or until lightly browned and fruit is tender.

Serving suggestion:

Serve warm with ice cream or milk.

Aunt Annabelle's Fruit Cobbler

Shirley Unternahrer
Wayland, IA

Makes 12 servings

Prep. Time: 15–20 minutes ⚜ *Baking Time: 40–50 minutes*

Nonstick cooking spray or butter to grease baking dish

6 cups diced rhubarb, blueberries, blackberries, or cherries

2½ cups sugar, divided

2 cups plus 2 tablespoons all-purpose flour, divided

1 teaspoon salt

⅓ cup canola oil

2 teaspoons baking powder

1 cup milk

2 tablespoons flour

Scant 2 cups boiling water

1. Grease a 9×13-inch baking dish. Spread the fruit across the bottom of the prepared baking dish.

2. In a mixing bowl, mix 1 cup sugar, 2 cups flour, and the salt, oil, baking powder, and milk. Mix until smooth.

3. Pour the mixture evenly over the fruit.

4. Mix the remaining 1½ cups sugar with the remaining 2 tablespoons flour.

5. Sprinkle the mixture over dough.

6. Slowly and evenly pour the boiling water over the top. Do not stir!

7. Bake at 375°F for 40 to 50 minutes, until lightly browned.

Variation:

You can use fruit such as peaches, but then reduce fruit amount to 5 cups instead of 6.

Quick Fruit Cobbler

OVEN

Lena Mae Janes
Lane, KS

Makes 6 servings

Prep. Time: 15 minutes ⚘ *Baking Time: 30 minutes*

⅔ cup sugar

1 cup flour

⅛ teaspoon salt

2 teaspoons baking powder

¼ cup milk

1 stick (½ cup) margarine or butter, melted

Nonstick cooking spray or butter to grease baking dish

21-ounce can fruit pie filling, any kind

1. In a medium-sized mixing bowl, mix the sugar, flour, salt, baking powder, and milk.

2. Add the melted butter and mix well.

3. Grease an 8×8-inch baking dish. Put the pie filling in the bottom of the prepared baking dish.

4. Pour the batter evenly over the pie filling.

5. Bake at 350°F for 30 minutes.

Tips:

1. Serve warm or cold. Top it with ice cream or whipped topping.
2. This is a good last-minute dessert when unexpected company comes and you want to serve a dessert.

Any-Fruit-That-Makes-You-Happy Cobbler

Phyllis Good
Lancaster, PA

Makes 6–8 servings

Prep. Time: 15–20 minutes ❧ Cooking Time: 1½–3 hours ❧ Ideal slow-cooker size: 3- or 5-qt.

Butter to grease slow-cooker crock

8 tablespoons (1 stick) butter

1 cup flour

1 cup milk

1 cup sugar, or less, depending on the sweetness of the fruit you're using

2 teaspoons baking powder

Dash salt

3–4 cups sliced fresh fruit, pitted cherries, or fresh berries

Variation:

Use whatever fruit is in season. Use more than is called for if you wish. You may need to cook it a bit longer, but this recipe is highly flexible.

1. Grease the interior of a slow-cooker crock. This mixture will fit into 3-, 4-, and 5-qt. cookers, whichever you have. The cobbler will be deeper in a 3-qt. than in a 5-qt., if that matters to you.

2. Melt the butter in a microwave-safe bowl. Stir in all the other ingredients except the fruit. Mix thoroughly.

3. Spoon the batter into the prepared slow-cooker crock, spreading it out evenly.

4. Arrange the fruit, cherries, or berries on top of the batter.

5. Cover. Bake on High for 1½ to 3 hours, depending on the fruit. It's finished when the middle is set and juice is bubbling at the edges.

6. Uncover, being careful not to let the condensation on the interior of the cooker lid drip on the cobbler.

7. Let cool until it's the temperature you like.

Cheesecakes

Mascarpone Cheesecake

Becky Lumetta
Romeo, MI

Makes 12 servings

Prep. Time: 35 minutes ⚜ *Baking Time: 99–130 minutes* ⚜ *Cooling Time: 6–8 hours*

Nonstick cooking spray or butter to grease springform pan

Crust:

1½ cups graham cracker crumbs (about 12 full cracker sheets crushed)

⅓ cups brown sugar

6 tablespoons melted butter

Filling:

16 ounces cream cheese at room temperature

1 cup sugar

1 teaspoon vanilla extract

10½ ounces mascarpone cheese at room temperature

2 eggs at room temperature

½ cup heavy cream at room temperature

1. Prepare a 9-inch springform pan by lightly greasing the bottom and sides, then lining the sides only with parchment paper if desired. (This will make it much easier to remove the cake from the pan.)

2. Preheat the oven to 350°F.

3. Mix all the crust ingredients. Pour into the prepared pan and press firmly into the bottom of the pan. Bake for 9 to 10 minutes. Cool completely while making filling.

4. Preheat the oven to 300°F. Place rack in bottom third of oven.

5. Place the prepared springform pan on a baking sheet.

6. It is best to have all ingredients at room temperature before beginning the next step, or warm them *carefully* in the microwave just before mixing, taking care not to melt the cheeses. For the eggs, warm them by gently by soaking in a bowl of warmish water before cracking. In the bowl of a stand mixer using paddle attachment (or with hand mixer) beat the cream cheese until smooth, stopping to scrape side of bowl and paddle multiple times. (Note: You can take as long as you need for this step, but make sure there are no lumps before adding any other ingredients. It will take longer the colder the cheese is. After other ingredients are added, attempts to remove lumps will incorporate air into your batter, which will result in a cheesecake that rises during baking and then settles and cracks while it cools.)

7. Scrape the bowl and paddle, add the sugar, and beat on low until the sugar is incorporated.

8. Scrape the bowl again, and add the vanilla and ⅓ of the mascarpone.

9. Scrape the bowl and paddle, and add another ⅓ of the mascarpone.

10. Scrape the bowl and paddle, and add the final ⅓ of the mascarpone.

11. Scrape the bowl and paddle, and add the eggs.

12. Scrape the bowl and paddle, and add the heavy cream.

13. Take the bowl off the mixer and scrape the paddle with a spatula.

14. Gently pour filling into the crust in the prepared pan.

15. Bake until the cake barely jiggles when the pan is tapped, about 90 to 120 minutes.

16. Allow to cool completely on a cooling rack then refrigerate overnight.

Cheesecake

Sharon Shank
Bridgewater, VA

Makes 8 servings

Prep. Time: 15 minutes & Cooling Time: 2–3 hours

2 tablespoons cold water

I envelope unflavored gelatin

2 tablespoons lemon juice

½ cup whole milk, heated almost to boiling

I egg

½ teaspoon liquid stevia

I teaspoon vanilla extract

2 cups cottage cheese

Lemon zest, optional

1. In a blender, combine the water, gelatin, and lemon juice. Process on low speed for 1 to 2 minutes to soften the gelatin.

2. Add the hot milk, processing until the gelatin is dissolved.

3. Add the egg, stevia, vanilla, and cottage cheese to the blender. Process on high speed until smooth.

4. Pour into a 9-inch pie plate or round flat dish.

5. Refrigerate for 2 to 3 hours.

6. If you wish, top with grated lemon zest just before serving.

Note:

This recipe is keto-friendly!

Choose Your Flavor Cheesecake

OVEN

Rhonda Freed
Croghan, NY

Makes 8 servings

Prep. Time: 15 minutes ⚶ *Cooking/Baking Time: 50 minutes* ⚶ *Cooling Time: 15 minutes*

2 (8-ounce) packages cream cheese, softened

3 eggs

1 cup sugar, divided

2 teaspoons vanilla extract, divided

1 cup sour cream

Pie filling of your choice, optional

1. In a large mixing bowl, beat the softened cream cheese, eggs, ¾ cup sugar, and 1 teaspoon vanilla with an electric mixer until smooth.

2. Pour into a 9-inch glass pie plate.

3. Bake at 350°F for 35 minutes on the second-to-bottom rack of the oven.

4. Remove from the oven and cool 15 for minutes. (Do not turn the oven off.)

5. In a small bowl, beat together the sour cream, ¼ cup sugar, and 1 teaspoon vanilla with electric mixer.

6. Pour over the top of the cake.

7. Bake at 350°F for 15 more minutes.

8. Cool completely. Store in refrigerator.

9. If you wish, top with the pie filling of your choice to serve.

Lemon Cheesecake

Meg Suter
Goshen, IN

Makes 8 servings

Prep. Time: 20–25 minutes   ❧   Baking Time: 60–65 minutes
Standing Time: 1 hour   ❧   Chilling Time: 2–24 hours

1¼ cups crushed graham crackers (about 10 whole crackers)

¾ cups crushed gingersnaps (about 15 cookies)

¼ cup sugar

5 tablespoons buttery spread

Nonstick cooking spray or butter to grease springform pan

4½ teaspoons egg substitute

6 tablespoons water

24 ounces nondairy cream cheese, softened and cut in small cubes

1 cup sugar

½ teaspoon vanilla extract

4–6 tablespoons fresh lemon juice

2 tablespoons lemon zest

Fresh strawberries for serving, optional

1. In a food processor, crush the graham crackers and gingersnaps. Add the sugar and buttery spread. Pulse until mixed.

2. Press into a lightly greased 9-inch springform pan.

3. Bake the crust at 350°F for 10 minutes, until golden. Set aside to cool.

4. Using an electric hand mixer in a large bowl, whip the egg substitute and water together until thick and creamy.

5. Beat in the cream cheese for 30 seconds—don't go longer!

6. Beat in the sugar, vanilla, lemon juice, and lemon zest just until smooth. Don't overbeat—this will cause cracking on the surface during baking.

7. Pour the batter into the crust. Smooth the top with a spatula.

8. Bake at 350°F, until center barely jiggles when pan is tapped, for 50 to 55 minutes. It is fine if it puffs up a bit and turns golden brown; it will settle as it cools.

9. Cool completely in pan on rack for at least one hour.

10. Refrigerate for at least 2 hours, but preferably 24 hours, before serving. This is lovely garnished with strawberries when ready to serve.

Blueberry Cheesecake

Betty Moore
Avon Park, FL

Makes 8 servings

Prep. Time: 10 minutes   &   *Cooking/Baking Time: 25–30 minutes*   &   *Chilling Time: 4 hours*

8 ounces cream cheese, softened

½ cup sugar

2 eggs, beaten

1 graham cracker crust

21-ounce can blueberry pie filling

1. Preheat oven to 325°F.

2. In a mixing bowl, combine the cream cheese, sugar, and eggs. Beat with an electric mixer until fluffy.

3. Pour mixture into the piecrust.

4. Bake for 25 to 30 minutes. Cool

5. Spread with half of the blueberry pie filling. Chill for 2 to 3 hours before serving.

6. Pass the remaining pie filling with the wedges of pie for anyone who wants to add more topping.

Variation:

Use any flavor of pie filling that you wish.

Creamy Orange Cheesecake

Jeanette Oberholtzer
Manheim, PA

Makes 10 servings

Prep. Time: 15 minutes ⚬ Cooking Time: 2½–3 hours
Standing Time: 1–2 hours ⚬ Chilling Time: 2–4 hours

Ideal slow-cooker size: large enough to hold your baking insert

Crust:

¾ cup graham cracker crumbs

2 tablespoons sugar

3 tablespoons melted butter

Filling:

2 (8-ounce) packages cream cheese, at room temperature

⅔ cup sugar

2 eggs

1 egg yolk

¼ cup frozen orange juice concentrate

1 teaspoon orange zest

1 tablespoon flour

½ teaspoon vanilla extract

1. Combine the crust ingredients in a small bowl. Pat into a 7-inch or 9-inch springform pan, whichever size fits into your slow cooker.

2. In a large mixing bowl, cream together the cream cheese and sugar. Add the eggs and egg yolk. Beat for 3 minutes.

3. Add the juice, zest, flour, and vanilla. Beat for 2 more minutes.

4. Pour the batter into the crust. Place on a rack (or jar rings) in the slow-cooker crock.

5. Cover. Cook on High for 2½ to 3 hours. Turn off and let stand for 1 to 2 hours, or until cool enough to remove from cooker.

6. Cool completely before removing sides of pan. Chill before serving.

Serving suggestion:

Serve with thawed frozen whipped topping and fresh or mandarin orange slices.

Chocolate Chip Cheesecake

Chris Kaczynski,
Schenectady, NY

Makes 16 servings

Prep. Time: 15 minutes & Baking Time: 45–50 minutes & Chilling Time: 3–4 hours

3 eggs, beaten

¾ cup sugar

3 8-ounce packages cream cheese, softened

1 teaspoon vanilla extract

24-ounce roll refrigerated chocolate chip cookie dough

1. Preheat oven to 350°F.

2. Place all the ingredients except the cookie dough in a large mixing bowl. With an electric mixer, blend until creamy. Set aside.

3. Slice the cookie dough into ¼-inch-thick slices. Set aside 9 slices.

4. Lay the remaining slices in the bottom of 9×13-inch baking dish. Pat the slices together to form a solid crust.

5. Spoon in the cream cheese mixture. Spread out over the cookie crust.

6. Arrange the reserved nine cookie slices on top of cream cheese mixture.

7. Bake at 350°F for 45 to 50 minutes. Allow to cool to room temperature.

8. Chill in refrigerator. When firm, cut into squares.

9. If you wish, when serving, top with whipped cream or chocolate topping.

Instant Pot Cookies & Cream Cheesecake

Hope Comerford
Clinton Township, MI

Makes 6 servings

Prep. Time: 15 minutes ⚭ Cooking Time: 35 minutes ⚭ Setting: Manual
Pressure: High ⚭ Release: Natural then Manual

Crust:

Nonstick cooking spray

12 whole gluten-free chocolate sandwich cookies, crushed into crumbs

2 tablespoons salted butter, melted

Cheesecake:

16 ounces cream cheese, room temperature

½ cup sugar

2 large eggs, room temperature

1 tablespoon gluten-free all-purpose flour

¼ cup heavy cream

2 teaspoons pure vanilla extract

8 whole gluten-free chocolate sandwich cookies, coarsely chopped

Toppings:

1 cup whipped cream

8 whole gluten-free chocolate sandwich cookies, coarsely chopped

Chocolate sauce, optional

1. Tightly wrap in foil the bottom of a 7-inch springform pan. Spray the inside with nonstick cooking spray.

2. In a small bowl, stir together the 12 crushed gluten-free chocolate sandwich cookies and melted butter. Press the crumbs into the bottom of the prepared pan. (I find the bottom of a glass cup is a great tool to use for this.) Place this in the freezer for 10 to 15 minutes.

3. In a large bowl, beat the cream cheese until smooth. (You can use an electric mixer, or a stand mixer with paddle attachment.)

4. Add the sugar and mix until combined.

5. Add the eggs, one at a time, making sure each is fully incorporated before adding the next. Be sure to scrape down the bowl in between each egg.

6. Add in the flour, heavy cream, and vanilla and continue to mix until smooth.

7. Gently fold in the 8 chopped gluten-free chocolate sandwich cookies and pour this batter into the pan you had in the freezer.

8. Cover the top of the pan with a piece of foil.

9. Pour 1½ cups of water into the inner pot and place the trivet in the bottom of the pot.

10. Create a "foil sling" by folding a 20-inch long piece of foil in half lengthwise 2 times. This "sling" will allow you to easily place and remove the springform pan from the pot.

11. Place the cheesecake pan in the center of the sling and carefully lower the pan into the pot. Fold down the excess foil from the sling to ensure the pot closes properly.

12. Lock the lid into place and make sure the vent is at sealing. Press the Manual button and cook on high pressure for 35 minutes.

13. When the Instant Pot beeps, hit the Keep Warm/Cancel button to turn off the pressure cooker. Allow the pressure to release naturally for 10 minutes and then do a quick release to release any pressure remaining in the pot.

14. Carefully remove the lid. Gently unfold the foil sling and remove the cheesecake from the pot to a cooling rack using the foil sling "handles." Uncover the cheesecake and allow it to cool to room temperature.

15. Once the cheesecake has cooled, refrigerate it for at least 8 hours, or overnight.

16. Before serving, top with whipped cream, chopped gluten-free chocolate sandwich cookies, and a drizzle of chocolate sauce if desired.

No-Bake Raspberry Cheesecake

Arlene M. Kopp
Lineboro, MD

Makes 10–12 servings

Prep. Time: 30 minutes ⚬ Chilling Time: 4–5 hours

3-ounce package raspberry gelatin

1 cup boiling water

8-ounce package cream cheese, softened

1 cup sugar

1 teaspoon vanilla extract

1⅓ cups (19–20 crackers) graham cracker crumbs

¼ cup melted butter

3 tablespoons lemon juice

12-ounce can evaporated milk, chilled

1. Place a large mixing bowl in the refrigerator. (You'll need it later to whip the milk.)

2. In a small bowl, combine the gelatin and boiling water, stirring until the gelatin is dissolved. Cool.

3. In a medium-sized mixing bowl, cream together the cream cheese, sugar, and vanilla. Mix well.

4. Add the gelatin. Mix well. Chill until it begins to set.

5. In a small bowl, combine the graham cracker crumbs and butter. Press ⅔ of the crumbs into the bottom of a 9×13-inch pan.

6. Combine the lemon juice and milk in the bowl you've been chilling. Whip until it is stiff and holds a peak.

7. Lightly fold the gelatin mixture into the whipped mixture.

8. Pour into the crumb crust in the pan, being careful not to disturb the crumbs. Sprinkle the top with the remaining crumbs.

9. Chill until set, about 2 to 3 hours.

Tortes, Tarts, and More

Chocolate Praline Torte

Edna Good
Richland Center, WI

Makes 14–16 servings

Prep. Time: 35 minutes ❧ *Baking Time: 35–40 minutes* ❧ *Standing Time: 1 hour*

1 cup brown sugar

1 stick (½ cup) butter

2 cups heavy whipping cream, divided

Nonstick cooking spray or butter to grease cake pans

¾ cup chopped pecans

18¼-ounce package chocolate cake mix

¼ cup confectioners' sugar

¼ teaspoon vanilla extract

Chocolate curls, optional

Tip:

Purchased whipped topping can be substituted for the topping ingredients in this recipe.

1. In a saucepan, combine the brown sugar, butter, and ¼ cup cream. Stir over low heat just until butter is melted.

2. Grease 2 9-inch round cake pans. Divide the mixture evenly between the prepared pans. Sprinkle with the pecans. Set aside.

3. Prepare the cake mix according to the package directions. Divide the batter evenly between the 2 pans, pouring carefully over the pecan mixture.

4. Bake at 325°F for 35 to 40 minutes or until a toothpick inserted in the center of the cake comes out clean.

5. Cool in pans for 10 minutes. Invert onto wire racks and carefully remove cakes from pans to cool completely.

6. Make the topping when the cakes are cool. For topping, beat remaining 1¾ cups cream in mixing bowl until soft peaks form. Gradually add the confectioners' sugar and vanilla, beating until stiff.

7. Place one cake layer, pecan-side up, on serving plate. Spread with half of the cream topping.

8. Place the second cake layer on top and spread with remaining topping. Top with chocolate curls, if desired.

Almond Pear Torte

OVEN

Martha Mullet
Sugarcreek, OH

Makes 8 servings

Prep. Time: 20–25 minutes ⚹ *Cooking/Baking Time: 20 minutes*

9-inch unbaked piecrust

¾ cup plus 2 teaspoons sugar, divided

3 tablespoons all-purpose flour

4 cups sliced peeled fresh pears (about 4 medium-sized pears)

3 tablespoons sliced almonds

1. Roll out piecrust into a 10-inch circle. Fold lightly into quarters, and place on an ungreased baking sheet with sides. (The sides are important in case the pastry develops a tear and the filling leaks out while baking.)

2. In a small bowl, combine ¾ cup sugar and the flour.

3. Add the pears. Toss to coat.

4. Place the pear mixture in the center of the pastry, spreading to within 2 inches of edges. Fold the edges up and slightly crimp.

5. Sprinkle with the remaining sugar.

6. Bake at 450°F for 15 minutes, or until the pears are tender.

7. Sprinkle with the almonds. Bake for 5 minutes longer.

8. Cool slightly before cutting into wedges.

Blueberry Torte

Jane Geigley
Lancaster, PA

Makes 3 servings

Prep. Time: 30 minutes ⚘ *Cooking Time: 2–3 hours* ⚘ *Ideal slow-cooker size: 3-qt.*

12 crushed graham crackers
4 tablespoons butter, melted
¾ cup sugar, divided
8 ounces cream cheese, softened
2 eggs
1 can of blueberry pie filling

1. Mix the graham crackers, butter, and ¼ cup sugar.

2. Press the mixture into the a slow-cooker crock.

3. Mix the cream cheese, ½ cup sugar, and eggs until smooth.

4. Spread on top of the graham crackers.

5. Pour the blueberry filling over the top.

6. Cover and cook on High for 2 to 3 hours.

Serving suggestion:
Serve warm with vanilla ice cream.

Blueberry Ginger Tart

SLOW-COOKER

Phyllis Good
Lancaster, PA

Makes 8 servings

Prep. Time: 30 minutes & Cooking Time: 1½–2 hours
Standing Time: 30–60 minutes & Ideal slow-cooker size: 6-qt.

I cup whole wheat pastry flour

¾ cup all-purpose flour

¼ cup brown sugar

⅛ teaspoon salt

⅔ cup butter, chilled

2 tablespoons fresh lemon juice, divided

3½ cups fresh or thawed and drained frozen blueberries

⅔ cup sugar

4 teaspoons cornstarch

I tablespoon finely grated lemon zest

2 teaspoons minced fresh ginger root

1. In a mixing bowl, stir together both the flours, the brown sugar, and the salt

2. Cut in the cold butter with 2 knives or a pastry blender.

3. Remove 1 cup of crumbs and set aside for topping. To the remainder in the bowl, add 1 tablespoon lemon juice.

4. Press the lemon crumb mixture into slow-cooker crock to make a tart crust that comes 1 inch up the sides.

5. Separately, stir together the blueberries, sugar, cornstarch, remaining 1 tablespoon lemon juice, the lemon zest, and the ginger.

6. Pour the filling into the tart crust. Sprinkle with reserved 1 cup crumbs.

7. Cover the slow cooker, venting lid at one end with wooden spoon handle or chopstick.

8. Cook on High for 1½ to 2 hours, until the blueberry filling is thickened and bubbling at edges.

9. Remove the crock from the cooker and uncover. Allow to cool for 30 to 60 minutes before slicing and serving.

Tip:

This is a wonderful combination of flavors. Be warned, however, that the slices will be gooey and tender, so don't expect perfect presentation. But the flavor will win you over!

Cherry Cheesecake Tarts

Jan Mast
Lancaster, PA

Makes 18 servings

Prep. Time: 15 minutes & Baking Time: 15–20 minutes

18 vanilla wafers
8 ounces cream cheese, softened
3 eggs
¾ cup sugar
21-ounce can cherry pie filling

1. Fill 18 cupcake tins with paper cupcake liners.

2. Place a vanilla wafer in each paper liner. Set aside.

3. Beat the cream cheese just until soft and smooth. Do not overbeat.

4. Add the eggs and sugar, beating until just blended. Do not overbeat.

5. Pour the cream cheese mixture evenly into 18 cupcake liners, covering vanilla wafer.

6. Bake at 325°F degrees for 15 to 20 minutes. Cool completely.

7. Top each cooled tart with cherry pie filling.

Tips:

1. Substitute blueberry pie filling or eliminate pie filling and use slices of assorted fresh fruits like kiwi, orange, strawberry, etc.

2. Refrigerate after preparing.

Peach Pecan Delight

Sue Hamilton
Benson, AZ

Makes 4 servings

Prep. Time: 10 minutes ❦ Cooking Time: 1½ hours ❦ Ideal slow-cooker size: 2-qt.

Nonstick cooking spray

15-ounce can sliced peaches with the juice

3.4-ounce box instant vanilla pudding mix, divided

12 pecan shortbread cookies, broken

4 tablespoons butter, melted

1. Spray the slow-cooker crock with nonstick spray.

2. Pour the peaches into the prepared slow-cooker crock. Add 4 tablespoons of the instant pudding and stir it in.

3. In a bowl, combine the broken cookies and the butter. Stir until well mixed.

4. Add the rest of the dry pudding mix to the cookie mixture. Spoon the mixture evenly on top of the fruit.

5. Cover and cook on High for 1½ hours.

Serving suggestion:
Serve warm with whipped cream.

Lemon Pear Gingerbread Delight

SLOW-COOKER

Sue Hamilton
Benson, AZ

Makes 6 servings

Prep. Time: 5 minutes ❧ *Cooking Time: 3 hours* ❧ *Ideal slow-cooker size: 7-qt.*

Nonstick cooking spray
21-ounce can of lemon cream pie filling
29-ounce can of sliced pears, drained
14½-ounce package of gingerbread cake and cookie mix
16 tablespoons (2 sticks) butter, cold

1. Spray the slow-cooker crock with nonstick cooking spray.

2. Spread the lemon filling in the bottom of the prepared slow-cooker crock.

3. Put a layer of the sliced pears over the filling.

4. Sprinkle the cookie mix on top of the fruit.

5. Cut the butter in slices and put on top of the mix.

6. Cover and cook on High for 3 hours.

Serving suggestion:

Let cool for 30 minutes before serving. Serve warm—or even better, ice cold.

Low-Carb Baking Powder

Hope Comerford
Clinton Township, MI

Makes 3 tablespoons

Prep. Time: 3 minutes

1 tablespoon baking soda
2 tablespoons cream of tartar

1. Mix baking soda and cream of tartar and store in an airtight container.

Metric Equivalent Measurements

If you're accustomed to using metric measurements, I don't want you to be inconvenienced by the imperial measurements I use in this book.

Use this handy chart, too, to figure out the size of the slow cooker you'll need for each recipe.

Weight (Dry Ingredients)

1 oz		30 g
4 oz	¼ lb	120 g
8 oz	½ lb	240 g
12 oz	¾ lb	360 g
16 oz	1 lb	480 g
32 oz	2 lb	960 g

Slow Cooker Sizes

1-quart	0.96 l
2-quart	1.92 l
3-quart	2.88 l
4-quart	3.84 l
5-quart	4.80 l
6-quart	5.76 l
7-quart	6.72 l
8-quart	7.68 l

Volume (Liquid Ingredients)

½ tsp.		2 ml
1 tsp.		5 ml
1 Tbsp.	½ fl oz	15 ml
2 Tbsp.	1 fl oz	30 ml
¼ cup	2 fl oz	60 ml
⅓ cup	3 fl oz	80 ml
½ cup	4 fl oz	120 ml
⅔ cup	5 fl oz	160 ml
¾ cup	6 fl oz	180 ml
1 cup	8 fl oz	240 ml
1 pt	16 fl oz	480 ml
1 qt	32 fl oz	960 ml

Length

¼ in	6 mm
½ in	13 mm
¾ in	19 mm
1 in	25 mm
6 in	15 cm
12 in	30 cm

Extra Information

Assumptions

flour = unbleached or white, and all-purpose

oatmeal or oats = dry, quick or rolled (old-fashioned),unless specified

pepper = black, finely ground

salt = table salt

shortening = solid, not liquid

spices = all ground, unless specified otherwise

sugar = granulated sugar (not brown and not confectioners')

Equivalents

dash = little less than ⅛ tsp.

3 teaspoons = 1 Tablespoon

2 Tablespoons = 1 oz.

4 Tablespoons = ¼ cup

5 Tablespoons plus 1 tsp. = ⅓ cup

8 Tablespoons = ½ cup

12 Tablespoons = ¾ cup

16 Tablespoons = 1 cup

1 cup = 8 oz. liquid

2 cups = 1 pint

4 cups = 1 quart

4 quarts = 1 gallon

1 stick butter = ¼ lb.

1 stick butter = ½ cup

1 stick butter = 8 Tbsp.

Beans, 1 lb. dried = 2–2½ cups (depending upon the size of the beans)

Bell peppers, 1 large = 1 cup chopped

Cheese, hard (for example, cheddar, Swiss, Monterey Jack, mozzarella), 1 lb. grated = 4 cups

Cheese, cottage, 1 lb. = 2 cups

Chocolate chips, 6-oz. pkg. = 1 scant cup

Coconut, 3-oz. pkg., grated = 1 cup, lightly filled

Crackers, graham, 12 single crackers = 1 cup crumbs

Crackers (butter, saltines, snack), 20 single crackers = 1 cup crumbs

Herbs, 1 Tbsp. fresh = 1 tsp. dried

Lemon, 1 medium-sized = 2–3 Tbsp. juice

Lemon, 1 medium-sized = 2–3 tsp. grated rind

Mustard, 1 Tbsp. prepared = 1 tsp. dry or ground mustard

Oatmeal, 1 lb. dry = about 5 cups dry

Onion, 1 medium-sized = ½ cup chopped

Pasta: Macaronis, penne, and other small or tubular shapes, 1 lb. dry = 4 cups uncooked

Noodles, 1 lb. dry = 6 cups uncooked spaghetti, linguine, fettucine, 1 lb. dry = 4 cups uncooked

Potatoes, white, 1 lb. = 3 medium-sized potatoes = 2 cups mashed

Potatoes, sweet, 1 lb. = 3 medium-sized potatoes = 2 cups mashed

Rice, 1 lb. dry = 2 cups uncooked

Sugar, confectioners', 1 lb. = 3½ cups sifted

Whipping cream, 1 cup un-whipped = 2 cups whipped

Whipped topping, 8-oz. container = 3 cups

Yeast, dry, 1 envelope (¼ oz.) = 1 Tbsp.

Index

About the Author

Hope Comerford is a mom, wife, elementary music teacher, blogger, recipe developer, public speaker, Young Living Essential Oils essential oil enthusiast/educator, and published author. In 2013, she was diagnosed with a severe gluten intolerance and since then has spent many hours creating easy, practical, and delicious gluten-free recipes that can be enjoyed by both those who are affected by gluten and those who are not.

Growing up, Hope spent many hours in the kitchen with her Meme (grandmother), and her love for cooking grew from there. While working on her master's degree when her daughter was young, Hope turned to her slow cookers for some salvation and sanity. It was from there she began truly experimenting with recipes and quickly learned she had the ability to get a little more creative in the kitchen and develop her own recipes.

In 2010, Hope started her blog, *A Busy Mom's Slow Cooker Adventures*, to simply share the recipes she was making with her family and friends. She never imagined people all over the world would begin visiting her page and sharing her recipes with others as well. In 2013, Hope self-published her first cookbook, *Slow Cooker Recipes 10 Ingredients or Less and Gluten-Free*, and then later wrote *The Gluten-Free Slow Cooker*.

Hope became the new brand ambassador and author of Fix-It and Forget-It in mid-2016. Since then, she has brought her excitement and creativeness to the Fix-It and Forget-It brand. Through Fix-It and Forget-It, she has written *Fix-It and Forget-It Healthy Slow Cooker Cookbook*, *Forget-It Healthy 5-Ingredient Cookbook*, *Fix-It and Forget-It Instant Pot Cookbook*, *Fix-It and Forget-It Plant-Based Comfort Foods Cookbook*, *Fix-it and Forget-It Keto Plant-Based Cookbook*, *Welcome Home Harvest Cookbook*, and many more.

Hope lives in the city of Clinton Township, Michigan, near Metro Detroit. She has been happily married to her husband and best friend, Justin, since 2008. Together they have two children, Ella and Gavin, who are her motivation, inspiration, and heart. In her spare time, Hope enjoys traveling, singing, cooking, reading books, spending time with friends and family, and relaxing.